I0438924

Columbia River Estuary Ecosystem Classification— Concept and Application

By Charles A. Simenstad and Jennifer L. Burke, University of Washington; Jim E. O'Connor and Charles Cannon, U.S. Geological Survey; Danelle W. Heatwole and Mary F. Ramirez, University of Washington; Ian R. Waite and Timothy D. Counihan, U.S. Geological Survey; and Krista L. Jones, Lower Columbia River Estuary Partnership

Prepared in cooperation with the University of Washington and the Lower Columbia River Estuary Partnership

Open-File Report 2011-1228

U.S. Department of the Interior
U.S. Geological Survey

U.S. Department of the Interior
KEN SALAZAR, Secretary

U.S. Geological Survey
Marcia K. McNutt, Director

U.S. Geological Survey, Reston, Virginia: 2011

For more information on the USGS—the Federal source for science about the Earth, its
natural and living resources, natural hazards, and the environment, visit http://www.usgs.gov
or call 1-888-ASK-USGS.

For an overview of USGS information products, including maps, imagery, and publications,
visit http://www.usgs.gov/pubprod

To order this and other USGS information products, visit *http://store.usgs.gov*

Suggested citation:
Simenstad, C.A., Burke, J.L., O'Connor, J.E., Cannon, C., Heatwole, D.W., Ramirez, M.F., Waite, I.R., Counihan, T.D.,
and Jones, K.L., 2011, Columbia River Estuary Ecosystem Classification—Concept and Application: U.S. Geological
Survey Open-File Report 2011-1228, 54 p.

Contents

Figures

Tables

Conversion Factors

SI to Inch/Pound

Multiply	By	To obtain
Length		
centimeter (cm)	0.3937	inch (in.)
meter (m)	3.281	foot (ft)
kilometer (km)	0.6214	mile (mi)
kilometer (km)	0.5400	mile, nautical (nmi)
meter (m)	1.094	yard (yd)
Area		
square meter (m^2)	10.76	square foot (ft^2)
square kilometer	0.3861	square mile
hectare (ha)	0.003861	square mile (mi^2)
Volume		
cubic meter (m^3)	6.290	barrel (petroleum, 1 barrel = 42 gal)
cubic meter (m^3)	264.2	gallon (gal)
cubic meter (m^3)	0.0002642	million gallons (Mgal)
cubic centimeter (cm^3)	0.06102	cubic inch (in^3)
Flow rate		
cubic meter per second (m^3/s)	70.07	acre-foot per day (acre-ft/d)
cubic meter per year (m^3/yr)	0.000811	acre-foot per year (acre-ft/yr)
meter per second (m/s)	3.281	foot per second (ft/s)
meter per year (m/yr)	3.281	foot per year ft/yr)
cubic meter per second (m^3/s)	35.31	cubic foot per second (ft^3/s)
cubic meter per day (m^3/d)	35.31	cubic foot per day (ft^3/d)
cubic meter per day (m^3/d)	264.2	gallon per day (gal/d)
cubic meter per second (m^3/s)	22.83	million gallons per day (Mgal/d)
cubic meter per hour (m^3/h)	39.37	inch per hour (in/h)
millimeter per year (mm/yr)	0.03937	inch per year (in/yr)

Specific conductance is given in microsiemens per centimeter at 25 degrees Celsius (µS/cm at 25°C).
Concentrations of chemical constituents in water are given either in milligrams per liter (mg/L) or micrograms per liter (µg/L).

Datums

Vertical coordinate information is referenced to the insert datum name (and abbreviation) here, for instance, "North American Vertical Datum of 1988 (NAVD 88)"
Horizontal coordinate information is referenced to the insert datum name (and abbreviation) here, for instance, "North American Datum of 1983 (NAD 83)"
Altitude, as used in this report, refers to distance above the vertical datum.

Columbia River Estuary Ecosystem Classification: Concept and Application

By Charles A. Simenstad, Jennifer L. Burke, Jim E. O'Connor, Charles Cannon, Danelle W. Heatwole, Mary F. Ramirez, Ian R. Waite, Timothy D. Counihan, and Krista L. Jones

Executive Summary

This document describes the concept, organization, and application of a hierarchical ecosystem classification that integrates saline and tidal freshwater reaches of estuaries in order to characterize the ecosystems of large flood plain rivers that are strongly influenced by riverine and estuarine hydrology. We illustrate the classification by applying it to the Columbia River estuary (Oregon-Washington, USA), a system that extends about 233 river kilometers (rkm) inland from the Pacific Ocean. More than three-quarters of this length is tidal freshwater. The Columbia River Estuary Ecosystem Classification ("Classification") is based on six hierarchical levels, progressing from the coarsest, regional scale to the finest, localized scale: (1) Ecosystem Province; (2) Ecoregion; (3) Hydrogeomorphic Reach; (4) Ecosystem Complex; (5) Geomorphic Catena; and (6) Primary Cover Class. We define and map Levels 1-3 for the entire Columbia River estuary with existing geospatial datasets, and provide examples of Levels 4-6 for one hydrogeomorphic reach. In particular, three levels of the Classification capture the scales and categories of ecosystem structure and processes that are most tractable to estuarine research, monitoring, and management. These three levels are the (1) eight hydrogeomorphic reaches that embody the formative geologic and tectonic processes that created the existing estuarine landscape and encompass the influence of the resulting physiography on interactions between fluvial and tidal hydrology and geomorphology across 230 kilometers (km) of estuary, (2) more than 15 ecosystem complexes composed of broad landforms created predominantly by geologic processes during the Holocene, and (3) more than 25 geomorphic catenae embedded within ecosystem complexes that represent distinct geomorphic landforms, structures, ecosystems, and habitats, and components of the estuarine landscape most likely to change over short time periods.

Introduction

We describe the rationale, conceptual basis, and application of a hierarchical ecosystem classification for large-river, flood-plain estuaries, and provide examples from the application of this controlling factor approach for the Columbia River estuary (Oregon-Washington, USA). A number of estuarine, delta and river-flood plain classifications based on geomorphology, hydrology, and salinity have been proposed as spatial frameworks for research and management (Hume and others, 2007). Few, however, completely integrate the estuarine to freshwater gradients or address the varying scales of geologic history and contemporary regional climate, watershed, ocean, riverine, and anthropogenic development factors that control estuarine ecosystem distributions and processes.

The Columbia River Estuary Ecosystem Classification (hereafter "Classification") described here addresses four prominent inconsistencies or gaps in existing estuarine ecosystem classifications and their application. These gaps are: (1) management applications (particularly in the USA) still tend to exclude significant tidal freshwater reaches of large-river estuaries, tidal flood (surge) plains, and deltas despite scientific recognition of the continuum of estuarine ecosystems from tidal saline to tidal fresh waters (see definition of 'estuary' below) and classifications that incorporate this breadth in estuary structure and processes; (2) focus by research and management efforts on the response attributes (for example, water quality, biota) rather than the 'controlling factors' and geological and hydrological processes that account for the occurrence, variation, and trends and patterns in change of ecosystem types driven by estuary and watershed characteristics and processes (although, see Hume and others, 2007); (3) little incorporation of large-scale and long-term "antecedent" processes, especially landscape modifying disturbance events, that over recent geologic time have shaped unique features of estuarine landscapes; and (4) no differentiation among features of estuarine landscapes and their component ecosystems that are formed by natural processes and those formed primarily by specific water and land-use management actions. Although we have attempted to address these needs specifically for the Columbia River estuary, we recognize that many of these inconsistencies continue to constrain the classification of large-river estuaries into ecosystem units that are useful for science and management decision-making in other systems around the world (McLusky and Elliott, 2007).

Our emphasis on the biophysical characteristics of ecosystems, factors that structure their occurrence and organization in estuaries, and consideration of regional to local scales of formative processes conforms with the more comprehensive definition of estuary from geological and geomorphological evidence that includes tidal freshwater reaches extending to the upper limit of tidal influence (Dionne, 1963; Dalrymple and others, 1992). Strong rationale for the initial geological and geomorphological perspective also has emerged from geochemical (Fairbridge, 1980) and biological disciplines (Schuchardt and Schirmer, 1991). Accordingly, we follow Perillo's (1995, p. 26) inclusive definition of estuaries that embraces physical and biological attributes and includes complex, hierarchical forms of estuaries:

> "An estuary is a semi-enclosed coastal body of water that extends to the effective limit of tidal influence, within which sea water entering from one or more free connections with the open sea, or any other saline coastal body of water, is significantly diluted with fresh water derived from land drainage, and can sustain euryhaline biological species from either part or the whole of their life cycle."

We adopt the definition of 'head of tide' that references water-level fluctuations affected by the tidal wave, which in turn influences shoreline and surgeplain vegetation and fauna assemblages because of their sensitivity to the regularity of water-level inundation and exposure. In adopting the head of tide as the ecotone between fluvial and estuarine ecosystems, we emphasize that more than just dilution of seawater by freshwater or current reversal structures the gradient from oceanic to fluvial ecosystems. Interactions of tidal and river forcing modulates hydrological, geomorphological, geochemical, biological, and ecological processes across the tidally influenced freshwater ("tidal freshwater") of lower watersheds in significantly different ways than in free-flowing fluvial ecosystems (for example, Schuchardt and others, 1993; Perillo, 1995; Elliott and McLusky, 2002; McLusky and Elliott, 2004; Wolanski, 2007). Whereas the European Communities Water Framework Directive's definition of "transitional waters" includes "partially saline in character" (European Communities, 2000), the concept of transitional waters across the European Union has been applied more pragmatically as "aquatic areas which are neither fully open coastal nor enclosed or flowing freshwater areas" where boundaries may be defined by physiographic features and discontinuities, or by salinity or any other hydrogeographic feature" (McLusky and Elliott, 2007). Thus, the broad concept of transitional waters is attentive to distinctions and "discontinuities" among ecosystem transitions where tidal and fluvial processes interact and is similar to the more modern definition of estuaries.

In this analysis, we also adhere to the ecological literature's distinction between "ecosystem" and "habitat" where an ecosystem is viewed as a community of plants, animals and micro-organisms and their abiotic environment interacting as an ecological unit whereas a habitat is a type of biotic and abiotic environment in which an organism (possibly specific to life history stage) lives. Because these terms are applied quite interchangeably in the conservation resource management literature, many 'habitat classifications' would likely fall into the category of ecosystem classification.

This initial summary provides the rationale and utility for the Classification and our approach to its design concepts and methods. We define the six hierarchical levels of ecosystem function and structure underlying the Classification. With this structure, we delineate the three broadest levels for the entire Columbia River estuary with existing geospatial datasets. For finer levels of the Classification, we provide examples of application for a single hydrogeomorphic reach. We also suggest potential science and management applications for the Columbia River estuary.

Impetus for New Estuarine Ecosystem Classification

The need to recognize how controlling factors influence the organization of estuarine ecosystems may be most effectively addressed by understanding the hierarchy of spatial and temporal scales over which the formative processes operate (O'Neill and others, 1986; Klijn and Udo de Haes, 1994; Hume and others, 2007). The complex and dynamic nature of ecosystems presents challenges when attempting to characterize their structure and function at one, manageable scale; even more so when the features and processes of interest span multiple temporal and spatial scales. Increasing the challenge of characterization is that ecosystems tend to be self-organizing. However, the concept of a hierarchy in ecosystems suggests that it may be tractable to delineate boundaries and that the transition in ecosystem processes across these boundaries may be meaningful to science and management (Gonzalez, 1996).

In conceptualizing the Columbia River Estuary Ecosystem Classification, we surveyed the published literature, unpublished and other "gray" reports and the World Wide Web (WWW) for existing classification schemes possibly appropriate for application to the Columbia River estuary. Examination of commonly utilized riverine and wetland classifications, and especially those including hydrological and geomorphological descriptors (for example, Leopold and Wolman, 1957; Bovee, 1982; Rosgen, 1994; Sear and others, 2003) indicated that they seldom approached tidal freshwater regions of watersheds. Some classifications explicitly consider tidal freshwater and tidal flood-plain ecosystems, although these tend to originate from Europe, Australia, New Zealand, and Asia and most have not yet reached peer review publication. For instance, the Water Ecotope Classification (WEC) originated in The Netherlands (Van der Molen and others, 2003) and adopts a classification that comprehensively bridges watersheds and coastal waters with "transitional waters" and is based on morphodynamics, hydrodynamics, and land use. In WEC, flood-plain ecotopes are defined, however, the resolution of these ecotopes is not detailed enough for delineation of biotic habitats. In fact, application of the European Union's (EU) Water Directive definition of "transitional waters" remains muddied around the differentiation between brackish and estuarine among broad seas, closed lagoons, or tidal estuaries (McKlusky and Elliott, 2007). Other estuary classifications (for example, Hume and Herdendorf, 1988; Simons and others, 2001) also include tidal freshwater and tidal flood plain ecosystems but do not classify estuarine features at the resolution of ecosystems. Although many recent approaches (for example, National Coastal/Marine Classification Standard for North America; Madden and Grossman, 2004) were developed to resolve deficiencies and inconsistencies in earlier classifications of habitat units and local structures for the estuarine and nearshore marine systems (Cowardin, 1979; Dethier, 1990; Brown, 1993; Wieland, 1993; Connor, 1997; Allee and others, 2000; Madley, 2002), none of these extended into tidal fluvial ecosystems and few provided much insight into tidal flood-plain ecosystems. However, Madden and Grossman (2004) make strong arguments for the need and mechanisms to link the National Coastal/Marine Classification Standard for North America to compatible freshwater classifications.

The large areas, high water velocities, and complex ecological interactions in large flood-plain rivers present substantial challenges to data gathering for comprehensive estuary classification. Hydraulic models are the basic tool for quantifying the interplay between hydrology and geomorphology and describing the physical aquatic habitat template. Hydraulic models have been used in the analysis and modeling of large rivers (Tiffan and others, 2002; Garland, 2004), but substantive differences in area, data requirements, and types of analyses dictate different approaches for using this tool on large rivers. For example, large rivers may stress computational resources for digital hydraulic models, and complex flow hydraulics around engineered structures and at the confluence of tributaries will require investigation of fine-scale enhancements and the utility of 2- and 3-dimensional models. At the same time, large rivers also offer opportunities to use high-resolution hydro-acoustic depth, velocity, and substrate-sensing instrumentation, new topographic data techniques such as Light Detection And Ranging (LiDAR), and extensive telemetry efforts that can provide datasets with high density and precision.

Many of these methods and data sources have been applied to estuarine classification at varying spatial and temporal scales. Although typical land-cover classifications based on remote sensing imagery (for example, Coastal Change Analysis Program [C-CAP] using LANDSAT imagery) are excellent tools for capturing ecosystem status and change at a particular spatial scale, they do not necessarily capture larger landscape-scale features that account for some of the inherent diversity of estuarine ecosystems. Furthermore, it would be desirable to capture indicators of the more dynamic features of estuaries (such as bars and tidal channels), where strong fluvial and tidal forces interact and structure complex landscapes and frequent natural and anthropogenic disturbances continuously modify and re-arrange landscape structure. Efforts to characterize dynamic, large-scale estuaries may benefit from a comprehensive classification that is based primarily on ecosystem-forming processes. Capturing the status and trends of landscape-scale features can be particularly important when it is desirable for research and management to examine and manage transitions and connectivity among habitats of organisms with migratory life histories such as anadromous fishes.

Large rivers typically are affected by alterations to hydrologic and geomorphic processes. Flow regimes of large rivers frequently are altered by reservoir regulation or water diversions. As such, restoration of the historical hydrograph often has been suggested as a primary action to restore ecosystem functions (National Academy of Sciences, 1992; Poff and others, 1997). This view assumes that the natural flow regime will return most, if not all, of the river's physical habitat template. However, large rivers also are characterized by extensive physical alterations of channel morphology due to navigation, flood protection, flood-plain drainage, and bank stabilization structures. These features control the distribution of water and sediment and strongly influence physical features, thereby altering geomorphic adjustments of the river system (Gore and Shields, 1995; Jacobson and Galat, 2006). Additionally, the development of dams on large-rivers systems alters the sediment transport regime, further influencing the river's ability for geomorphic adjustments (Bayley, 1995; Syvitski and others, 2005a; Jacobson and others, 2009). Hence, the restoration of a natural hydrograph alone is unlikely to restore all physical features of large rivers unless other factors affecting hydrologic and geomorphic processes such as dikes and levees also are addressed. Much of the practical management of large rivers involves informed tradeoffs between hydrology and geomorphology, a decision-making process that can be guided by the relative ecological benefits and societal costs of altering these characteristics.

The Columbia River estuary exemplifies both the need and the challenges in classifying complex ecosystem structure along steep environmental gradients controlled by broad-scale regional tectonic and geologic processes, contemporary seasonally and annually variable hydrology and sedimentology, and even more rapid ecological responses. Flow regulation by the hydropower system and major alterations in channel configuration (for example, construction of dikes and levees and dredging to maintain the mainstem navigation channel) characterize present constraints on ecosystem-sustaining processes in the Columbia River estuary. For instance, loss of access to the natural flood plain and connectivity between habitats by the construction of levees has been implicated in habitat loss for juvenile salmon (*Oncorhynchus* spp., 13 populations of which are listed under the Endangered Species Act), both within the lower estuary (Thomas, 1983) and in tidal freshwater regions (Kukulka and Jay, 2003b).

In developing a strategy for a comprehensive ecosystem classification scheme appropriate to the entire tidally influenced region of the Columbia River estuary (fig. 1), we drew on the limited existing approaches to classifying and assessing functionality of large rivers, coastal flood plains, and estuaries. More than three-quarters of the length of the Columbia River estuary is tidal freshwater. Potentially at least 155 km of the 230 km estuary was historically exposed to effective tidal action (Syvitski and others, 2005b). Regulated flows have augmented dry-season discharges resulting considerably more persistent tidal freshwater under current conditions (Sherwood and others, 1990; Simenstad and others, 1992). This is particularly relevant to the existing need for an ecosystem classification scheme because tidal freshwater regions, particularly of large tidal flood plain rivers such as the Columbia River, are seldom included in the currently accepted classifications for either estuaries or rivers. Although land-cover classifications routinely include tidal freshwater vegetation and other unique surface features, hydrological, geomorphological, or landscape features are seldom included.

In presenting this classification, we recognize that it is an *a priori* approach at the levels (resolutions in hierarchy) which we found unresolved in most estuarine classifications. At this interim stage of the Classification, we have had no opportunity or mechanism to validate the more unique classes. By putting this forward, however, we invite rigorous, scientific testing of the Classification as a valid framework for the characterization and organization of estuarine ecosystems and as a management tool. In the Discussion, we present some examples of how the Classification could be, and is actually being tested and applied.

Objectives

Given the general lack of a documented estuarine ecosystem classification that met the setting and research and management needs of large-river and flood-plain estuaries such as the Columbia River estuary, we drew upon estuary classification literature (see prior discussion, particularly Perillo's 1995 comprehensive synopsis) and designed a hierarchical framework that would delineate useful classes across different scales of the diverse ecosystems and component fish and wildlife habitats. The primary purpose of the classification is to promote and facilitate systematic research, monitoring, and management of diverse ecosystems. We place particular emphasis on ecosystems that encompass the important fish and wildlife habitats that are much of the management focus in the Columbia River estuary. The Classification is, however, designed to provide a more utilitarian framework for understanding the underlying ecosystem processes that create the dynamic structure of the Columbia River and other, comparable large-river and coastal flood plain estuaries that possess extensive transitions and ecotones from tidal freshwater to euhaline ecosystems. As such, it is intended to assist scientists and managers who seek a broader scale of understanding required to study, manage, and restore these transitional ecosystems.

Approach

Columbia River Estuary, Processes and Ecosystems

Commensurate with the spatial extent of the Columbia River estuary, the geographic scope of the Classification (fig. 1) extends from the outer mouth (the oceanic end of the jetties) to the upstream extent of tidal variability in water level, which for the contemporary system is the downstream base of Bonneville Dam (about rkm 233); although the tidal wave is a minor component of the water-level fluctuation at this point, it is still distinguishable, particularly at low flow. This location also is close to the historical extent of tidal influence at the lower end of now-inundated Cascade Rapids. The lateral extent is defined as encompassing all elevations from deepest channel depths to the upper elevations of the historical flood plain, as well as flood plains of the tidally affected extent of tributary rivers. At present, we tentatively delineate the current flood plain as encompassing surfaces as high as 18 mm above North American Vertical Datum of 1988. The mapped floodplain extent will change during the process of mapping for the Classification as we refine our understanding of Holocene geology, flood-plain morphology, and early pre-settlement flood elevations (based on U.S. Army Corps of Engineers, 1968; Kukulka and Jay, 2003a, 2003b). The rationale for encompassing the entire area of the historical flood plain is that we intend the Classification to enable (a) comparison with historical ecosystem structure and (b) evaluation of restoration scenarios that may involve re-inundation of mainstem and tributary flood plains.

The geologic history provides insight into the events that created the physiographic template for the estuary. Our interpretations of contemporary ecosystem structure originate from understanding of Quaternary geologic processes and events as well as of currently active processes. As should be evident in the descriptions of the features that define at least five of the six levels in the Classification, large-scale, geologic and tectonic processes are responsible for much of the template for ecosystem structure in the estuary.

Setting of the Columbia River Basin and Estuary

The Columbia River drains 660,480 km^2 of western North America, flowing 2,000 km from its headwaters at Columbia Lake in southeastern British Columbia, Canada, to its confluence with the northeast Pacific Ocean near Astoria, Oregon. In terms of drainage area, the Columbia River is the 39th largest river basin in the world (Vorosmarty and others, 2000), but it ranks higher with respect to mean discharge (23rd of primary rivers entering seas or oceans), mean elevation (7th of largest 50 rivers entering seas or oceans; Vorosmarty and others, 2000), and slope (5th of largest 50 rivers entering seas or oceans; Vorosmarty and others, 2000). By discharge volume, the Columbia River is the largest river to enter the northeast Pacific Ocean and conveys 77 percent of the total runoff from western North America (Hickey, 1998). The basin drains several physiographic regions, including the middle and northern Rocky Mountains, Columbia Plateau, Cascade Range, and Pacific border (Fenneman and Johnson, 1946). The basin includes parts of British Columbia, Canada, most of Idaho, large parts of Oregon and Washington, and small areas of Montana, Wyoming, Utah, and Nevada. The estuary forms the border between Washington and Oregon and traverses the Portland-Vancouver metropolitan area. Within the Columbia River estuary, the river crosses the Cascade Mountains and Pacific border provinces.

The Columbia River drainage basin is unique among the world's largest rivers in that it drains toward the leading edge of a convergent tectonic margin. This setting is responsible for the relatively high basin elevation and mean channel slope. More specifically, this unique environment has a great effect on the lower river and estuary, where processes such as volcanism, seismicity, and mass movements significantly influence fluvial processes and the geomorphology of the river corridor. As discussed in more detail when we describe the Classification, the spatial and temporal scales of formative geologic processes and events correlate strongly with the proposed Classification, with broader subdivisions chiefly owing to tectonism and volcanism over the last 50 million years (Ma), and finer subdivisions primarily affected by processes and landscape history of the last 20,000 years. At the finest scales, modern and historical geologic, hydrologic, and ecologic processes exert primary influence.

Columbia River Basin hydrology reflects the interaction of topography resulting from the regional geologic environment and history, and the regional moist, maritime climate. Most Columbia River discharge is the product of Pacific frontal systems moving east with the mid-latitude westerlies, with most precipitation falling as winter snowfall in the Rocky Mountains and in the Cascade Range. Mean annual river discharge at the mouth is about 6,970 m^3/s) (Naik and Jay, 2005). Approximately 24 percent of this volume originates from west of the Cascade Range crest, despite a contributing area totaling only 8 percent of the river basin (Sherwood and others, 1990). Most of this discharge enters by the principal tributaries, the Willamette and Cowlitz Rivers, which drain large parts of the Puget-Willamette forearc trough. The hydrologic imbalance between east and west of the Cascade Range owes to the rainy Maritime climate of the western Cascade Range and Pacific border provinces, where average annual runoff is 2.39 m; by contrast, the interior subbasin with its Middle Latitude Steppe climate yields only about 0.71 m/yr (U.S. Army Corps of Engineers, North Pacific Division, 1984).

Historically, mean monthly discharges at the mouth varied between late fall lows of about 3,500 m^3/s and May–June highs averaging about 15,000 m^3/s. Annual peak discharges almost always resulted from snowmelt in the interior subbasin and peaked at 35,100 m^3/s (estimated at The Dalles, Oregon; June 7, 1894). The lower basin typically does not add substantially to historical spring freshets, but has been a major contributor to large winter discharges on the Columbia River (Sherwood and others, 1990) and occasionally produced large (but typically short-duration) winter peaks on the lower estuary associated with regional rain-on-snow floods, such as those in December 1861 and December 1964.

Both eastern and western subbasins of the Columbia River basin are subject to climate variation driven by two cycles originating from the Pacific Ocean: (1) the El Niño-Southern Oscillation (ENSO) conditions in the equatorial Pacific that is associated with warm, wet climate in the Pacific Northwest every 3–8 years and cold, dryer climate ("La Niña") in the off-cycle (Ropelewski and Halpert, 1986); and (2) Pacific Decadal Oscillation (PDO), which is driven more by climate dynamics in the North Pacific Ocean and involves oscillating warm and dry climate eras every 20–30 years that is particularly manifest in cycling coastal ocean temperatures and biological productivity (Mantua and others, 1997). Both of these climate cycles are associated with hydrological and other climate disturbances that contribute to the dynamics of the Columbia River estuary's landscape.

Contemporary Hydrologic and Geomorphic Processes and Landforms

The geologic history of the Columbia River has produced the background of physical conditions and landforms with which historical and modern processes interact to continue to shape the channel and flood plain. Inputs, outputs, and transfers of water, sediment, and organic debris are the key attributes of the geomorphic system constituting the estuarine corridor of the Columbia River. By understanding how these exchanges work in the context of the geologic history, one can better understand how changes to geomorphic processes and conditions, either by natural or anthropogenic means, might affect the physical character of the lower river.

Floods and Tides

Flowing water exerts the fundamental force forming and altering most landforms of the estuary. As for most estuaries in this region, tidal forcing and basin runoff affect discharge direction, stage, and energy (Jay and others, 1990). River conditions, including stage and discharge energy, for the lowermost 21–56 km (depending on ambient discharge) are dominated by tidal forcing. In this reach, channel and flood-plain characteristics chiefly owe to tidal action. From rkm 21 to rkm 56, the estuary undergoes a transition characterized by a minimum in "energy flux divergence" associated with salinity intrusion (Jay and others, 1990). Up-estuary of the transition, fluvial forcing becomes more influential, and the landforms in the uppermost reaches primarily result from flood processes.

The tidal pattern affecting the estuary is mixed diurnal and semidiurnal, meaning two low and two high tides of unequal heights each lunar day (24.8 hours). Tidal amplitude ranges from 1.7 to 3.6 m at the ocean entrance, increasing to a maximum of 2.0 to 4.0 m near Astoria at rkm 29 before decreasing eastward to less than 0.2 m at Vancouver (rkm 171), but still affecting discharge stage at low river discharges as far upstream as Bonneville Dam at rkm 233 (Kukulka and Jay, 2003a). Tidal forcing has less effect when river discharge is extremely high; common historical flood discharges (for example, the June 1, 1946 discharge of 16,500 m^3/s) are tidally affected as far upstream as rkm 138, whereas the largest discharges are not measurably affected by tidal forcing upstream of Longview at rkm 106 (U.S. Corps of Engineers, 1968). Tidally forced current reversal penetrates to the Cowlitz River confluence at rkm 109 during periods of very low river discharge (Clark and Snyder, 1969), and saltwater intrusion as far upstream as rkm 37 (Fox and others, 1984). Tidal currents are strongest at the river entrance to the

Pacific Ocean, where discharge is constricted by jetties and between Clatsop Spit and Cape Disappointment, and decrease inland. Within the estuary, Neal (1972) reported surface currents greater than 3.3 m/s during ebb tides, and 2.0 m/s during flood tides.

Floods probably bring more kinetic energy to the estuary than any other source, and for most of the lower estuary, floods are the primary agent of geomorphic change. For the 1858–1941 period pre-dating significant discharge regulation in the basin, the mean peak Columbia River flood was 17,400 m^3/s. Judging from a profile of stages measured during the 1946 flood of 16,500 m^3/s (U.S. Army Corps of Engineers, 1968), floods of this magnitude have stages ranging from 8.8 to 3.0 m above the low water plane, with the greatest values being in the western Columbia River Gorge. The highest discharges of June 1894 and June 1948, both resulting from coincident snowmelt peaks from the upper Columbia and Snake River basins, had maximum stages as great as 13.4 m above low water (U.S. Army Corps of Engineers, 1968). The gradients of the flood profiles relate directly to discharge energy and dissipation. For all spring freshet flood profiles for the Columbia River estuary depicted on "U.S. Army Engineer District Portland Flood Profiles," encompassing discharges ranging from 16,500 to 35,100 m^3/s, the steepest water-surface slopes (except for the short reach just down estuary of Bonneville Dam) are between Kalama (rkm 120) and Westport (rkm 80) (Hydrogeomorphic Reaches C and D, see section, "Results"). Consequently, these reaches have the greatest fluvial energy of the lower estuary. Distinctly lower gradients encompass the reaches from Kalama to the western end of the Columbia River Gorge, reflecting hydraulic ponding up estuary from the narrowed valley at Kalama. Gradients also flatten down estuary of rkm 65, due to the expansion of the estuary.

Discharge conditions lead to three basic geomorphic environments as outlined by Jay and others (1990): (1) a zone between the river mouth and about rkm 8 (see Hydrogeomorphic Reach A, in section, "Results") in which hydraulic energy is dominated by dissipation of tidal currents; (2) the reaches upstream of rkm 56 (see Hydrogeomorphic Reaches C-G, in section, "Results") where fluvial energy dominates and little tidal energy persists; and (3) the intervening "energy flux divergence minimum" reach (the upstream part of Hydrogeomorphic Reach A and all of Reach B, in section, "Results") between the fluvial and tidal reaches where fluvial energy and tidal energy dissipation are both small (fig. 1). This categorization neatly organizes many of the geomorphic properties, discharge, and sediment movement in the lower estuary.

Sediment Movement and Transfers

Nearly all natural landforms within the flood-plain boundaries of the estuary are formed of clastic materials transported and deposited by the river. Most of this sediment is sand, silt, and clay. Most of the sediment along the lower river corridor comes from upstream or from tributaries entering the lower river; very little sediment enters the lower river from the ocean or by eolian transport from coastal beaches (Sherwood and Creager, 1990). From consideration of deposit volumes along the lower river, Gelfenbaum and others (1999) estimated that the long-term (about 10,000 years) sediment supply to the estuary has been about 20×10^6 m^3/yr), with about 75 percent of this sediment load exiting river for the Pacific Ocean. The balance of about 5×10^6 m^3/yr has filled the estuary valley as it has aggraded in conjunction with Holocene sea-level rise. From measurements and hindcasting, Gelfenbaum and others (1999) estimated that the historical (1879–1934) rate of sediment inflow was much lower, with only about 8.7×10^6 m^3/yr entering the estuary. Compared to other large U.S. rivers, the modern sediment load of the Columbia River is low—about one-tenth that of the Colorado River, and about 40 percent of the Mississippi River on a load per unit drainage area basis (Ritter, 1967). Similarly, very few world rivers have sediment loads as low as the Columbia River (Sundborg, 1983, as cited in Cooke and Doornkamp, 1990). Annual fluxes probably vary tremendously in conjunction with discharge. Hindcast estimates of annual transport rates range from more than 35×10^6 m^3/yr for the 1894 big-discharge year to less than 2×10^6 m^3/yr for some of the low-discharge years of the last 3 decades, when discharge peaks have been significantly regulated and sediments have accumulated behind dams (Gelfenbaum and others, 1999).

The sources of sediment to the estuary are distinctly segregated by area and size (Whetten and others, 1969). Areas upstream of the Cascade Range chiefly provide fine-grained (fine sand and finer) non-volcanic sediment whereas tributaries from the Cascade Range provide coarser sediment (chiefly sand) of andesitic volcanic origin (Whetten and others, 1969). Measurements by Hauschild and others (1966) indicate that the Snake River supplies substantially more sediment than the Columbia River at their confluence. The lower tributaries, in addition to providing most of the coarse component of the sediment load are also likely to provide a significant fraction of the total sediment load. Calculations summarized by Sherwood and others (1990) suggest that the Willamette River may contribute approximately 10 percent of the annual sediment load to the lower river.

Fluvial sediment transport is by two primary mechanisms—suspended and bedload. In the Columbia River and estuary, the suspended load consists primarily of the fine sand and finer materials supplied by the upper river basin (Whetten and others, 1969), but also at times including fine-grained material generated by Cascade Range volcanic eruptions (Hubbell and others, 1983). The coarser sediment—chiefly sand—moving on the bed is primarily volcanic rock fragments, presumably derived from the Cascade Range (Hauschild and others, 1966; Whetten and others, 1969). Suspended-load transport rates depend primarily on the volume of fine sediment introduced to the river system, which is primarily a function of watershed sediment supply processes. Bedload transport in the estuary is judged to be capacity-limited and is primarily a function of discharge strength, because much of the lower river channel is sand covered (Sherwood and others, 1990). Whetten and others (1969) estimated that bedload transport constitutes about 10 percent of the total sediment load, although few measurements support this conclusion. During high discharges, bed material can be entrained into suspension, leading to substantial sand transport in suspension (Hauschild and others, 1966). Suspended load constitutes the bulk of the sediment load of the estuary. Although about 75 percent of the suspended load is transported to the ocean (Gelfenbaum and others, 1999), the balance is deposited in aqueous and tidal environments such as peripheral bays and side channels (Sherwood and others, 1990), as well as on terrestrial surfaces such as flood plains and mid-channel islands subject to overbank flooding and deposition.

A large proportion of the bedload movement along the lower estuary is likely by migrating bedforms. Large sand waves and other channel bedforms along the estuary have been described by Hickson and Rodolf (1951), Jordan (1962), Hauschild and others (1966), Whetten and others (1969) and Sherwood and Creager (1990). Whetten and others (1969) mapped the lower river, noting that 45 percent of the channel between Bonneville Dam and the Willamette River confluence was covered in sand waves, with abundance increasing to 80 percent for the segment between the Willamette and Cowlitz River confluences, and 86 percent for the segment between the Cowlitz River and the ocean. Hauschild and others (1966) reported dunes in the Columbia River channel averaging 1.5 m high, and 30–90 m in length; dimensions slightly smaller than those described by Jordan (1962) near Longview, which had amplitudes averaging about 2 m, lengths of about 500 m, and average spacing of about 100 m. Smaller bedforms, primarily current ripples, are commonly superimposed on these large sand waves. Hauschild and others (1966) reported that the dunes in deeper parts of the channel evolved from long and low to short and high as discharge increased. Dune migration rate near Vancouver ranged from less than 1 m/d during low discharge periods, to as great as 60 m/d during high discharges (Hauschild and others, 1966). Bedform morphology in most of the lower Columbia River estuary indicates downstream transport, but reversing currents result in bidirectional bedform movement as far upstream as about rkm 25 (Sherwood and Creager, 1990).

Summarizing sediment and sediment transport conditions from several lines of reasoning and observation, Sherwood and Creager (1990) conclude:

1. "Virtually all of the sediment in the estuary is derived from the Columbia River."

2. "The lower estuary (see Hydrogeomorphic Reaches A and B, in Results) displays the most sediment-size variation because of the wide gradient of transport processes [fluvial to tidal] and depositional environments in the region."

3. "The absence of coarse sand in the entrance and lower estuary, and the general fining-seaward trend exhibited in sediment size, suggest that the coarsest fraction of the fluvial sediment is not being transported through the estuary." This observation, coupled with the Jay and others (1990) description of system energetics, leads to the strong probability that the region of the energy flux divergence minimum between rkm 21 and 56 is where most of medium and coarse sands is retained. Peterson and others (2003) refer to this region of active deposition in the Cathlamet Bay area as a "bay-head delta."

In addition, Whetten and others (1969) came to the conclusion, also supported by the analyses of Hauschild and others (1966), that the majority of suspended load to the Columbia River basin is derived from the upper basin, and most bedload to the Columbia River is derived from the Cascade Range, and that these two sediment populations remain distinct as they move through the lower river.

Design of Columbia River Estuary Ecosystem Classification

To develop a classification that captures the multiple and hierarchical scales of processes that influence estuarine ecosystems, we integrated information on riverine, oceanic, climatic and watershed factors that influence estuarine processes with information on geomorphic and biological features that vary across the estuarine gradient into a hierarchical framework classification. Similar to the "controlling factor" approach used in the Estuary Environment Classification (EEC) by Hume and others (2007), the Columbia River Estuarine Ecosystem Classification is based on systems hierarchy concepts (for example, O'Neill and others, 1986) and uses comparable proxies for regional, watershed, and estuarine ecosystem processes. This Classification extends into the tidal freshwater reaches of estuaries, thus addressing the EEC's limited applicability to large rivers and flood plain estuaries and classification of individual estuarine components (Hume and others, 2007).

Based on the structure of other classification schemes developed for estuarine ecosystems described earlier, and common concepts of ecosystem geography (for example, Bailey, 1996), we developed an ecosystem classification for the Columbia River estuary that is organized in six hierarchical levels:

Ecosystem Province
Ecoregion
Hydrogeomorphic Reach
Ecosystem Complex
Geomorphic Catena
Primary Cover Class

The Classification is designed to aggregate land and aquatic cover classes (including culturally modified land cover/land use classes and modifiers) according to the conceptualized ecosystem processes that structure landscape attributes, including biotic habitats at multiple spatial scales. The Classification methodology is based on digital geographic information systems (GIS), whenever possible using automated processes with minimal manual classification that facilitates an objective, repeatable, hydrogeomorphic class system. We use either scientifically based classification schemes that already exist for the area or develop rational rules adaptable to GIS-based analyses. Many data sources are readily available as GIS map layers. As these layers are updated and improved, they can be incorporated into revisions of the Classification methodology. In initially developing the Ecosystem Complex and Geomorphic Catena levels of the Classification, we have interpreted both digital and non-digital data (for example, cartographic geology) in order to delineate complexes and catenae.

Methods

Data Criteria and Requirements

We adopted the following primary and secondary selection criteria for the design of the classification and for selection of the data upon which it would be based.

Primary Criteria for Classification Design

> Datasets used to develop the Classification primarily will be contemporary, comprehensive, complete, and widely available.
>
> Landscape features must be mappable at appropriate scale to delineate important ecosystem components (cover types and shapes).
>
> Because the influence of geology, physiography, and climate on hydrogeomorphic process regimes accounts for much of the variation in ecological attributes we observe through the estuary (particularly the tidal freshwater regions), we use indicators of hydrogeomorphic processes to delineate the classification level (Level 3, Hydrogeomorphic Reaches) above those incorporating ecological features.
>
> The Classification will capture scale of ecosystem dynamics (for example, development stage of ecosystems) that are anticipated to indicate ecological change over likely monitoring scales.
>
> Finer scale levels of the Classification should capture ecosystem features that are indicative of habitat required by biota of concern (for example, species at risk, species listed as threatened or endangered).
>
> The Classification should incorporate features of relevance to landscape and disturbance ecology of large tidal flood plain estuaries.

Secondary

> Design should be enable delineation of some Classification levels using both historic spatial datasets and future spatial datasets.
>
> Application of the Classification to historic and future spatial datasets will facilitate ecosystem change analyses for multiple points in time.

GIS Structure

All GIS data in the Classification methodology are readily available from State and Federal government agencies (table 1). Although the classification relies primarily on contemporary data sources, we utilize historical data to support ecosystem change analyses for areas where both historical and contemporary datasets are available.

For the preliminary mapping at the finer levels of the Classification, GIS processing utilized ESRI ArcGIS 9.3 ArcInfo with the Spatial Analyst extension. All data layers were imported to a geodatabase and projected to the State of Oregon standard (Lambert Conformal Conic, NAD 1983 datum, meter map units) for processing consistency. Full implementation and reporting of the classification system and mapping will follow USGS standards for GIS products and associated metadata.

Base Data and Analytical Steps

Historical Flood Plain and Tidal Extent

The spatial extent of the Classification is defined by our interpretation of the boundaries of the Holocene flood plains and extent of tidal influence ("head of tide") in the estuary and tributaries. The limits of tidal influence up the Columbia River and for tributaries were determined using regional tidal elevation data (U.S. Army Corps of Engineers, 1968; Kukulka and Jay, 2003a) in combination with 10-m digital elevation models (DEMs). The limits of the flood plain were derived from our interpretation of the extent of Holocene flood plain deposits (based on high-resolution LiDAR topography existing geologic maps) in conjunction with documented historical flood elevations (U.S. Army Corps of Engineers, 1968).

Level-Specific Data Sources

The Classification has six levels; at the broadest scale, Levels 1 and 2 are derived from existing national scale ecologic classification systems and datasets and require only brief descriptions. The finer levels of Levels 3 through Level 6 are the aspects new to the proposed Classification and their source data and development are more fully described.

Levels 1 and 2— Ecosystem Province and Ecoregion

We selected the EPA-adopted Ecoregion Levels II and III to provide regional context at the highest levels of the hierarchy (Classification Levels 1, 2, and partially 3). These ecoregion delineations reflect the regional variability of watersheds, which plays a strong peripheral (if not cumulative) effect on the structure of estuarine ecosystems such as the Columbia. For example, vegetation compositions differ dramatically in the different physiographic provinces defined by Ecoregion Levels II and III (Sowa and others, 2007).

As initially developed by Bailey (1983, 1987, 1995), Bailey and others (1994), Omernik (1987, 1995), and Omernik and Bailey (1997), the ecoregion concept provides a broad-scale framework in which ecological regions are distinguished by patterns and the composition of abiotic and biotic phenomena, such as climate, geology, physiography, hydrology, vegetation, soils, land use, and wildlife. Although there may be similarities among some of these characteristics, the relative importance of each, and the interrelationship among them, varies across regions. To encompass the coarsest scales of influence on the estuary, we adopted without modification the EPA Ecoregion Level II (Ecosystem Province) as Classification Level 1, and EPA Ecoregion Level III (Ecoregion) as Classification Level 2.

The EPA Ecoregion II maps were derived through analysis of satellite imagery and appropriate natural resource source maps at small scales (approximately 1:40 million – 1:50 million) while Ecoregion III maps used similar resources to nest large ecological areas within Ecoregion Level II areas at a finer scale (approximately 1:20 million – 1:30 million) (Omernik, 1987, 1995; Omernik and Bailey, 1997).

The biophysical framework of the Columbia River basin and the estuary in particular represented by these two levels of the Classification has been established by tectonic, volcanic, climatologic, and biologic processes operating over the last 50 Ma. Key elements include formation and uplift of the Coast and Cascade Ranges, uplift of the Rocky Mountains, and development and growth of the Columbia River basin. This broad context is helpful for understanding the overall physiography of the lower Columbia River (including hydrological, geological, and ecological factors associated with tributaries), but it encompasses temporal and spatial scales typically too coarse to provide a meaningful framework for management, restoration, and monitoring.

Level 3—Hydrogeomorphic Reach

This level in the hierarchy diverges from the EPA ecoregion scheme, as well as other estuarine classifications, in order to incorporate indicators of ecosystem structure and process that encompass and assimilate tidal and freshwater controlling factors. To integrate watershed and tributary contributions and other influences with flood-plain processes and tidal-fluvial interactions along the estuarine gradient, and to recognize the importance of river network structure in classification hierarchy (Frissell and others, 1986; Rice and others, 2008), we adjusted the boundaries of EPA Level IV Ecoregions by incorporating tributary confluences, flood plain and other physiographic features and fluvial-tidal hydrologic and other discontinuities to delineate "hydrogeomorphic reaches" or Classification Level 3.

Five primary factors were used to determine locations of hydrogeomorphic reach boundaries progressively (up-estuary) along the estuarine gradient:

1. Maximum (historic) salinity intrusion: Oligohaline and brackish salinities drive distributions of aquatic biota, and are regions of important geochemical transitions through processes such as flocculation; we positioned the up-estuary extent of historical salinity (0–0.5 practical salinity units [psu]) based on Sherwood and others (1990);

2. Up-estuary excursion of estuarine turbidity maximum (ETM): Although associated with the incursion of salinity, the ETM is a lower estuary feature where dynamic sedimentation, geochemical and biological processes (particularly food web interactions between bacteria and zooplankton) are primarily concentrated in the mainstem channel but may interact with peripheral bay environments (Jay and others 1990; Baross and others, 1994; Jay and Musiak, 1994; Prahl and Coble, 1994; Reed and Donovan, 1994; Simenstad and others, 1994a, b; Small and Morgan, 1994; Crump and Baross, 1996; Morgan and others, 1997; Prahl and others, 1997; Crump and others, 1999; Fain and others, 2001). We used information from Simenstad and others (1994a&b; and unpublished data) to approximate the mean position of the ETM;

3. Up-estuary extent of current reversal: Much of the initial deposition of sediment, detritus and associated constituents that occurs in the mainstem estuary is associated with slack tide periods when particles have time to settle. Because this feature shifts daily and seasonally with discharge and tide levels, we adopted the mean position of the up-estuary extent of tidal reversal from predicted currents along the estuary using Tides & Currents Ver. 2.5, Nautical Software, Inc.;

4. Convergences with major tributaries and slough systems. These features are important sources of dissolved and suspended materials (for example, suspended sediment, large wood, and detrital matter from upstream watersheds); anecdotal evidence suggest that tributaries and sloughs support high densities of fish and wildlife and are important staging areas for anadromous juvenile and adult salmon and smelt. However, potentially toxic water-soluble contaminants may be found in higher concentrations around confluences, for example, Columbia River confluences with the Willamette River and Multnomah Channel (Fuhrer and others, 1996); and,

5. Transitions in maximum flood (pre-regulation) tide level: Maximum water elevation and the frequency and duration of flood events are major factors determining wetland community structure, particularly in the flooding disturbance regime in a tidal flood (surge) plain; we used flood profiles available for the length of the estuary to interpret major inflections in flood elevations due in part to marked changes in the elevation of the river bed and other channel morphology changes that affect conveyance (U.S. Army Corps of Engineers, 1968; Kukulka and Jay, 2003a, 2003b).

The level of the Hydrogeomorphic Reach in the Classification represents the intersection of broad-scale geologic processes and events over the last 50 Ma with more modern or recent geologic and hydrologic processes of the Holocene. The overall physiography of the reaches relates primarily to the broad-scale geologic environment, including the Cascade and Coast Ranges, and the Portland Basin, whereas many of the defining criteria such as current and tide conditions reflect modern and recent geological conditions and processes.

The Hydrogeomorphic Reach level is the coarsest level of the Classification that encompasses the entire flood plain, albeit for lengths of Columbia River (and major tributaries) of similar overall character as defined by the above criteria. Within the Columbia River estuary, overall flood-plain morphology is dominated by Holocene aggradation since the sea-level low about 15,000 years ago. This aggradation typically has resulted in the flood plain abutting older bedrock units, but in places the flood plain is flanked by Quaternary alluvium deposited by the ancestral Columbia River, deposits of large ice-age floods, and volcanogenic deposits from eruptions of nearby Mount Hood and Mount St. Helens (Evarts and others, 2009).

Level 4—Ecosystem Complex

Unlike the higher levels in the Classification, ecosystem complexes are biophysical patches formed by long-standing geologic and hydrologic processes that establish long-term geomorphic templates in the estuary and its flood plain in addition to continuous and more recent hydrologic and geomorphic processes that result in changing landscape mosaics of landform and vegetation patches. For the most part, the Ecosystem Complex category reflects geomorphic process regimes and episodic geologic events of the Holocene (last 10,000 years), resulting in landforms such as terraces, dune fields, flood plains, volcanogenic deltas, and channels. Thus, Ecosystem Complexes are influenced by the overlapping effects of massive Holocene disturbances (such as landslide and volcanic sediment pulses, large floods, storm surges, or tectonic movements), shorter-term biophysical processes (such as erosion and sedimentation associated with localized flooding, vegetation succession, local extinction and recruitment events), and anthropogenic modifications of the landscape (such as diking and filling, channel hardening, and urban and suburban development on the flood plain).

Numerous data sources (table 1) and GIS processes are used to derive Classification Level 4—Ecosystem Complex level of the Classification. Each hydrogeomorphic reach is evaluated and processed individually for complexes, building on basic GIS rules but with modifications commensurate with changes in geomorphic and ecosystem structure by hydrogeomorphic reach. The foundation of the Ecosystem Complex level was the delineation of major aquatic features of the estuary based on bathymetry, while the flood plain and other episodically and partly inundated features were based on interpretation of topographic, geologic and geomorphic features.

Complete mapping the Ecosystem Complexes across all reaches awaits full implementation of the Classification[1], but for purposes of describing the Classification, we show proposed ecosystem complexes for Hydrogeomorphic Reach F. This reach extends along the Columbia River's flood plain from (and including) the confluence of the Willamette River to the confluence of the Lewis River (fig. 1).

Ecosystem Complexes (table 2) within the aquatic domain (areas continuously submerged or typically submerged during the tidal cycle) were mapped by rule sets applied to bathymetric data: (1) Deep water channels were delineated where depths were greater than the fourth quartile of the entire bathymetry dataset (>8 m relative to North American Vertical Datum of 1988); and (2) Distributary channels were delineated where depths were greater than 1 m and less than 8 m.

Flood-plain Ecosystem Complexes required more interpretative mapping to distinguish landforms coinciding with various hydrologic and geomorphic process regimes (table 2). This mapping primarily was accomplished on the basis of topographic characteristics supported by existing geologic and soils mapping.

The Ecosystem Complexes (as well as features mapped at finer levels of the Classification) mapped for Hydrogeomorphic Reach F will not encompass all types of Ecosystem Complexes for the Columbia River estuary. We anticipate that most Hydrogeomorphic Reaches will have Ecosystem Complexes (as well as features at finer Classification levels) unique to that reach and that the total number of types of Ecosystem Complexes will be much larger for the Columbia River estuary. Similarly, application of the Classification for different fluvial estuary systems will certainly produce a different set of Ecosystem Complexes.

Level 5—Geomorphic Catena

Geomorphic catenae form the mosaic of physical and biological features nested within ecosystem complexes. Because both natural ecosystem processes and the intrinsic characteristics of catena vary and change over space and time, catenae occur in a 3-dimensional shifting mosaic of ecosystems along the river-ocean continuum (Stanford and others, 2005). In the Stanford and others (2005) typology, the Classification's ecosystem complexes tend to persist but can be constrained or eliminated by human alteration while the geomorphic catenae form the shifting mosaic that, "…changes spatially over time due to primary drivers, particularly flooding, channel avulsion, cut and fill alluviation (erosion and deposition of fine and coarse sediments), deposition of wood [, and] recruitment and regeneration of riparian vegetation." For the Columbia River estuary, Geomorphic Catenae consist chiefly of individual landforms created during the last 2,000 years since rate of sea-level rise diminished markedly (table 3). Examples of such landforms include individual bars, levees, islands and ponds. The

---

[1] Collection of high-resolution bathymetry data was completed in 2010, and classified land-cover data will be available in mid-2011, under the auspices of the Lower Columbia River Estuary Partnership (LCREP) and is being incorporated into delineation of the Ecosystem Complexes for all estuary reaches.

dynamics of these processes result in more temporal variation of landscape patches categorized at this level of the classification. At the Geomorphic Catena level, the Classification provides potential coastal flood plain and estuary classes that would extend the typologies proposed by Stanford (1998), Ward and others (2002), and Stanford and others (2005) to the sea.

Geomorphic catenae are classified and delineated in two steps: (1) within ecosystem complexes, multiple mapping criteria and sources are used to distinguish water body and flood-plain features occurring within each complex; and (2) Level 6—Primary Cover Class data are applied in conjunction with other geospatial data (for example, LiDAR) to delineate discrete biological communities associated with the geologic/geomorphic units delineated in step (1). In addition to bathymetry, the primary data sources for the first step included: (1) aerial photography; (2) topographic maps; (3) soils maps; and (4) geology maps; the primary sources for the second step included the LiDAR, bathymetry and LANDSAT land-cover data (table 1).

Level 6—Primary Cover Class

The Primary Cover Class Structure is the finest level of the hierarchical scheme. It includes the elements that compose spatial coverage of classes in the Classification Level 5—Geomorphic Catena. Although land cover is the highest resolution level of the Classification, we do not use it as the ultimate dependent variable in the hierarchy. Although land cover of natural ecosystems implies some level of equilibrium adjustment of vegetation communities to abiotic variables at a landscape scale, land cover of highly altered ecosystems is more static and provides less insight into the relationship between abiotic variables and vegetation (or absence thereof). For this reason, we used land cover selectively for two purposes: (1) to modify the least altered ("reference") conditions of abiotic catenae (table 3) to relate ecosystem responses and states to geologic and other physicochemical processes; and (2) identify cultural modifications that can inform restoration and management decisions for ecosystem rehabilitation and recovery. We are utilizing the most recently completed 2010 Lower Columbia River Estuary (LCRE) Land Cover Classification that was derived using a high resolution image segmentation and object based classification process that integrated data from: (1) 2009 4 band, 1 m resolution airborne imagery acquired by the USDA National Agriculture Inventory Program (NAIP); (2) archived 30 m LANDSAT TM5 imagery from various dates ranging from 2007 to 2009; and (3) 2009–10 LiDAR elevation data acquired by the U.S. Army Corps of Engineers (table 1). This classification was supported by extensive training data in some regions of the system. However, work is underway in the study area to provide an updated (for example, 2009–10) land-cover dataset to facilitate finer resolution catenae delineation for the completion of the Classification. In addition to cultural features (such as dikes, roads, fill, and other infrastructure) identified in the delineation of the geomorphic catenae, any artificial or otherwise modified Primary Cover Class (such as agricultural fields, park and other lawns) is additionally distinguished by a modifier. In the pilot example, 24 Primary Cover Classes are represented for Reach F.

Results

Each level of the Classification encompasses different scales of influence on ecosystem structure, where the highest levels in the scheme describe regional-scale structure and the lowest levels compose the finer scale components of the strata in the hierarchy levels. For example, each of the Geomorphic Catena in Level 5 is composed of sets of the Primary Cover Classes in Level 6. These sets or aggregations of cover classes are not necessarily unique other than their association with larger scale features (described below under Level 6—Primary Cover Class). Similarly, each Hydrogeomorphic Reach in Level 3 is composed of various compositions and arrangements of Ecosystem Complexes, which are expected to vary among the different reaches. Table 4 provides a framework for the classification hierarchy in relation to geology, time, and human disturbance.

We describe Levels 1 through 3 of the Classification for the entire estuary. Levels 4-5 are not complete because of incomplete bathymetry and land-cover data (Level 6) over the entire study area. As a demonstration, we present one hydrogeomorphic reach (Reach F) as an example of the potential delineations of features at the ecosystem complex and geomorphic catena scales.

Level 1—Ecosystem Province

As described in section, "Setting of the Columbia River Basin and Estuary," the Basin is distinctly divided by the Cascade Mountain Range into the warmer and wetter Marine West Coast Forest Province to the west and the drier Western Cordillera and Cold Deserts provinces to the east— east of the Range (fig. 2). Although the Marine West Coast Forest Province makes up only 8 percent of the Basin area, this Province contributes 24 percent of the fluvial forcing that differs in timing, magnitude, and constituents (for example, sediment, organic matter) relative to freshwater discharge from the large eastern region of the Basin [see Whetten and others (1969); Sherwood and others (1990); and Prahl and others (1998) for more detail about the various contributions from these different provinces to the estuary.]

Level 2—Ecoregion

Moving from the Columbia River estuary's mouth upstream to Bonneville Dam, the Coast Range Ecoregion extends more than100 km from the Pacific Ocean to Willamette River (fig. 3A). On the Washington side of the Columbia River, the Puget Lowland Ecoregion includes the Cowlitz River valley and influences about a 10 km length of the estuary at that river's confluence with the Columbia River near Longview, Washington. Along both the Oregon and Washington sides of the Columbia River, the Willamette Valley Ecoregion surrounds the broad flood-plain region of the lower Willamette River and its confluence with the Columbia River. Lastly, the Cascades Ecoregion extends from the beginning of the estuarine flood plain to the Columbia River Gorge and Bonneville Dam.

Level 3—Hydrogeomorphic Reach

The EPA's eight Level IV Ecoregions (fig. 3B) are the foundation of the Classification's Level 3-Hydrogeomorphic Reaches and relate to estuarine ecosystems primarily by the character and magnitude of fluxes of water, sediment, nutrient, contaminant, and other constituents delivered by tributaries draining different ecoregions. The EPA's Coast Range Ecoregion includes four more detailed ecoregions (the Coastal Lowlands, Coastal Uplands, Willapa Hills, and Volcanics). The larger Puget Lowland Ecoregion is distinct and does not include more detailed Ecoregions at the EPA's Level IV. Level III Willamette Valley Ecoregion is divided into two smaller Ecoregions, the Portland/Vancouver

Basin and Valley Foothills. At the western end of the Gorge, the Level III, Cascades Ecoregion includes the West Cascades Lowlands and Valleys Ecoregion and a tongue of the Valley Foothills Ecoregion.

Revising the EPA Level IV ecoregions based on additional hydrological and physiographic criteria (see Level 3—Hydrogeomorphic Reach in section, "Methods"), we delineated the following eight reaches (fig. 4; appendix A). For each of these Hydrogeomorphic Reaches, tentative flood-plain boundaries (as shown in figs. 1 and 4) were determined by a simple elevation criterion of 18 m above North American Vertical Datum of 1988. These floodplain boundaries will be refined, as they have been for Reach F (fig. 5), on the basis of mapping at Levels 4 (Ecosystem Complex) and 5 (Geomorphic Catana). For each reach, we summarize the dominant channel features, major geologic events, sediment inputs, and tidal influence.

1. *Coastal Lowlands Entrance-Mixing (rkm 0–23)*—Level IV Coastal Lowlands, encompassing euhaline salinities and the region of most extensive mixing of estuarine and ocean waters around the estuary's entrance and surrounding bays and tributary entrances. Broad mud and sand flats are particularly prominent features in the peripheral bays. This reach may have some of the most dynamic environmental conditions in terms of timing, frequency, and duration of disturbances. On regular and predictable tidal scales, factors like water salinity, velocity, and turbidity are affected by turbulent mixing of fluvial and oceanic waters across the estuary's entrance. More stochastic disturbance events also are accentuated at the fluvial-tidal interface, where high perigean tides, storm surges and fluvial flooding can produce extreme coastal flooding events that occur approximately once per decade (Pacific County Historical Society and Museum , 2000) despite the extensive flood control capacity of the Columbia River Basin hydrosystem. This region also experiences extreme coastal disturbances associated with periodic subduction zone earthquakes including tsunami and episodes of coseismic subsidence (2–3 m) following by tectonic uplift (Atwater and Hemphill-Haley, 1997). In addition to the massive subduction zone earthquake last experienced on January 26, 1700, more than 20 significant earthquakes and 12 tsunami have been reported in the vicinity of Astoria and Willapa Bay since 1840 (Pacific County Historical Society and Museum , 2000). As a result of coastal tectonics, this hydrogeomorphic reach continues to experience coastal uplift, resulting in an average sea level fall of 0.7 to 1.7 mm/yr (Burgette and others, 2009), partly offset by episodic subsidence during subduction zone earthquakes.

2. *Coastal Uplands Salinity Gradient (rkm 23–61)*—Level IV Coastal Uplands and Willapa Hills ecoregions combined, including the strongest salinity gradient from mesohaline to oligohaline at the up-estuary extent of salinity intrusion (about rkm 45). Through this reach, the estuary converges from open and peripheral bays and bay head delta into a confined fluvial valley. Perhaps the most unique feature of this reach is the broad, complex mosaic of mid-channel islands, shoals and distributary and tidal channels. Sea level fall continues in this reach, producing emergence of up to 1.2 mm/yr east of rkm 52 (Burgette and others, 2009). The combination of sea level fall and sediment accretion had produced 1–6 mm/yr of shoaling that is particularly evident in the "bay-head delta" of this reach (Sherwood and others, 1990; Peterson and others, 1999). As a result, successional development of sand and mud flats to emergent marshes, and emergent marshes to woody scrub-shrub and forested tidal wetlands appears to have occurred on islands in the reach (for example, Russian Island; Elliot 2004); conversely, very little erosion and disturbance is evident over the same period.

3. *Volcanics Current Reversal (rkm 61–103)*—although dominantly a fluvial environment, Level IV Volcanics Ecoregion encompasses most of the up-estuary extent of current reversal (to rkm 85 during low discharge): Reach C extends through a confined valley that bisects the eastern Coast Range but still contains large, swampy mid-channel islands, distributary channels and sloughs, and flood plains. Tidal influence diminishes extensively throughout the reach, such that the seasonal river discharge range at the eastern end of the reach is about 4.4 m but the maximum tidal influence is only 0.34 m. The primary natural disturbance regimes include energetic floods, downstream sediment deposition from episodic inputs from Mount St. Helens, and coastal subsidence from the massive subduction zone earthquakes up to about 80 rkm.

4. *Western Cascades Tributary Confluences (rkm 103–119)*—most of the Level IV Puget Lowland Ecoregion, including the confined valley along the mainstem river and the broad bottomlands at the confluences of the Cowlitz and Kalama Rivers. Back channels and tidal channels dissect the flood plains. The river current seldom reverses within this reach although there is still about 0.2 m range of tidal influence. This reach receives episodic sediment inputs from the watershed and tributaries up-estuary as well as volumetrically prominent pulses of volcanogenic sediments from Mount St. Helens eruptions that enter the estuary as sediment or lahars through the Cowlitz River and Kalama River valleys. In the last several centuries, Mount St. Helens has erupted multiple times producing large amounts of sediment from 1480 to 1482 and in 1980 when it released about 100×10^6 m^3 of sediment that entered the estuary by 1987 (Gates, 1994). Additionally, in this reach, un-diked islands and flood plains have actively accreting and eroding margins (Atwater, 1994), resulting in local bar-and-swale morphology on islands and flood plains (for example, Cottonwood Island; Carrolls Channel).

5. *Tidal Flood Plain Basin Constriction (rkm 119–137)*—up-estuary segment of Level IV Puget Lowland Ecoregion and lower segment of the Level IV Portland/Vancouver Basin, divided at the major constriction in the estuary's flood plain near the community of St. Helens and including the confluence of the estuary with the Lewis River: Other than the bottomlands formed at the confluences of the Lewis and Kalama Rivers, Reach E is narrowly confined by Tertiary bedrock valley sides and Pleistocene terrace and volcanic deposits. Both the Kalama and Lewis Rivers have conveyed volcaniclastic debris to the Columbia River from eruptions of Mount St. Helens, including large volume inputs about 2500 and 500 BP (Vogel, 2005). Tidal fluctuation has small influence (about 0.8 m range at Kalama), especially during peak flood stages of 7–9 m. Most of the flood plain islands, Columbia River flood plains and Lewis and Kalama Rivers deltas are thinly capped by fine sediments deposited from overbank flooding. Flood discharges have produced prominent channel migration bar-and-swale morphology on the islands and flood plains. The results of these processes are evident at Deer Island, where lateral bars and natural levees have formed from river migration during the late Holocene, leaving lower, swampy areas in the flood plain formed to the west.

6. *Middle Tidal Flood Plain Basin (rkm 137–165)*—portion of the Columbia and Willamette Rivers (including Multnomah Channel) flood plains in the Level IV Portland/Vancouver Basin down-estuary of the major confluence of the estuary with the Willamette River: This is the widest flood plain reach of the upper estuary where the wide alluvial valley (including Sauvie Island) is bounded by the Portland Hills uplift to the west and the Cascade volcanic arc to the east. The flood plain is composed of wetlands and many seasonal ponds within bar-and-swale deposits and scoured bedrock areas, as well as terraces and rocky outcroppings. Many of the wetland complexes are separated from the mainstem Columbia River channel by the slightly higher flood plain bar-and-swale deposits generated by lateral channel migration. The flood plain is circumscribed by distributary channels, most notably Multnomah Channel; many circuitous sloughs and tidal channels connect swale wetlands embedded in the bar-and-swale topography. Dikes, levees, road grades and drainage ditches have locally altered the hydrology and inundation characteristics of this reach. Tributary sediment delivery has not kept pace with the high rates of the Columbia River aggradation from downstream sedimentation, resulting in drowned tributary valleys, such as Scappoose Bay, that are integrated into the flood plain mosaic. Positioned downstream of the confluence of the Willamette and Columbia Rivers, this reach has been particularly vulnerable to flooding from combined Columbia River Basin freshets and coastal storms prior to completion of the substantial flood control capacity in the Willamette River basin during the mid- to late-20th century. Flooding from the "pineapple express" coastal storms (Colle and Mass, 2000) can influence this reach, including five floods of 3 m above Willamette River flood stage since 1876, with the most recent in 1996. This reach has little tidal influence, particularly during high river discharge.

7. *Upper Tidal Flood Plain Basin (rkm 165–204)*—portion of the Level IV Portland/Vancouver Basin from just upstream of the Willamette-Columbia Rivers confluence up-estuary to the western entrance to the Columbia River Gorge. Reach G is the up-estuary continuation of the wide alluvial valley centered around Holocene flood plain bounded by Pleistocene fluvial deposits and isolated Quaternary volcanic centers on the north and south. The Sandy and Washougal Rivers confluences in the eastern end of the reach are associated with narrow deltas and flood-plain wetlands. Sediment inputs from Mount St. Helens are primarily multiple limited-depth episodes of air-fall tephra deposition. Mount Hood, however, has been a large source of volcanogenic sediment, mainly by way of the Sandy River which joins the Columbia River at the upstream end of this reach. Mount Hood has erupted during two major periods since the 16th century, most recently from 1879 to about 1900, producing at least three lahars that entered the Columbia River about 1,500 years ago and depositing 340–640×10^6 m^3 within 15 km downstream of confluence (Rapp, 2005). Mid-channel islands (for example, Government, Reed Islands) appear to have been formed only in the last 500 years (Evarts and O'Connor, 2008), likely growing in a down-estuary direction from sediment deposition initiated by accumulations of large woody debris. Major portions of the flood plain have been modified by levees and fill, particular in North Portland. Tidal variability in water level generally is obscured by river freshets and daily power peaking cycles of Bonneville Dam.

8. *Western Gorge (rkm 204–233)*—Level IV West Cascades Lowlands and Valleys to Bonneville Dam: The terminal reach of the estuary is confined to the western end of the Columbia River Gorge, which was cut through the uplifted Cascade Range during the last 3–3.5 Ma (Evarts and others, 2009). The Holocene valley fill is locally flanked by Missoula Flood deposits and Pleistocene terraces, but much of the river is bordered by bedrock, coarse-grained alluvial fans, colluvium, and large landslide complexes, especially on the northern slopes (O'Connor and Burns, 2009). The few peripheral flood plains (for example, Franz Lake) and wetlands occur mostly in the downstream lee of rocky valley projections but not at the outlets of major tributaries as in other reaches (for example, Sandy River in Reach G). Many of the prominent mainstem features like the large islands (for example, Bradford, Hamilton, Pierce Islands) were formed by the breaching of the A.D. 1415–1445 Bonneville Landslide sometime before A.D. 1479, producing a peak discharge as great as 110,000 m^3/s and diverting the river channel south (abandoning the river course that is now Greenleaf Slough). This flood left distinctive overbank deposits down-estuary as far as Wallace Island in Hydrogeomorphic Reach C (Atwater, 1994; O'Connor, 2004; O'Connor and Burns, 2009). Evidence of late Holocene sand dune formation and growth over the last 2,500 years are still evident on Sandy Island and east of Rooster Rock. Steep valley walls provide episodic inputs of coarse-grained debris-discharge sediment, especially around the Warrendale area where large active fan complexes convey sediment from the steep walls of the Columbia River Gorge into the Columbia River. The influence of the tides (range less than 0.3 m) is much less than that of the power peaking cycle created by discharges from Bonneville Dam.

Level 4—Ecosystem Complex

At this time, complete mapping of ecosystem complexes throughout the entire Columbia River estuary has been limited by gaps in recent bathymetry datasets, which are a critical component for mapping aquatic ecosystem complexes. However, we here provide an example of ecosystem complexes for Hydrogeomorphic Reach F (fig. 5) where bathymetric and terrestrial data are mostly complete. The first step was refinement of the flood-plain boundary on the basis topographic, pedologic, and geomorphic criteria, resulting in a more accurate boundary encompassing the areas flanking the lower Willamette River and Columbia River subject to fluvial inundation, erosion, and deposition. Within this refined flood-plain in this reach, 16 classes of complexes were delineated. Primary complex classes are associated with flood-plain features, primary and tributary channels, and regularly flooded features. We delineate some natural features within the reach, such as rocky outcrops in the Holocene flood plain, which are never inundated (or essentially "terrestrial"). With the exception of landforms completely obscured by extensive modifications (the "Developed" class), we do not distinguish anthropogenic modifications of the system because they are assumed to be nested at finer scale within a complex; however, we recognize that in some cases, human modification may encompass an entire complex such as construction of dikes or levees around the perimeter of flood plain islands.

Ecosystem complexes in Reach F include six types of channels that are permanently flooded and three channel margins that are intermittently exposed (wetlands). The dominant features are flood plain and channel islands (four). As indicated in table 2, not all ecosystem complexes are represented in Hydrogeomorphic Reach F.

Level 5—Geomorphic Catena

Geomorphic catenae are individual landforms nested within Ecosystem complexes and consisting of distinctive Primary Cover Class types. Development of geomorphic catenae for the entire Columbia River estuary also is impeded at this time by missing datasets, such as bathymetry data for Level 4 and recent, complete land-cover data for Level 6 (see below, Level 6—Primary Cover Class). Here, we combined the Level 4–Ecosystem Complexes developed for Hydrogeomorphic Reach F and 2010 land-cover data to generate an initial delineation of geomorphic catenae for Reach F (fig. 6). We have identified 27 classes of geomorphic catenae in Reach F, including 4 aquatic classes (including the Unknown Depth class), 3 tributary or other channel classes (including Tributary Valley), 13 tidal flood plain classes, 5 artificial or developed (including Unknown) classes, and 2 relict classes (bedrock, terrace) that occur throughout the reach; 5 modifiers that distinguish extensive anthropogenic alterations.

Although many of the geomorphic catenae are discrete or slightly clustered (for example, terraces) other catenae are extensively interconnected. For instance, flood plain channels typically connect to lakes, marshes, and forests on flood plains. Similarly, as indicated in the hydrogeomorphic reach descriptions, flood plain bar, and scroll features are often associated with flood plain lake/ponds and herbaceous low marshes within the scroll features.

Unlike the ecosystem complexes, the classification and delineation of geomorphic catenae are more variable (and even ephemeral) because complexes are partially dependent on short-term, instantaneous "snap-shot" datasets such as aerial photography, LiDAR, and satellite remote sensing imagery. Catena classes that expand and contract with variable hydrologic conditions are the most vulnerable to this source of variation and mapping uncertainty.

Level 6—Primary Cover Class

The Level 6–Primary Cover Class data that we are using to integrate biological and other attributes with the geological and geomorphic features for Level 5–Geomorphic Catena in Reach F is based on integrated high resolution image segmentation and object based classification of NAIP and LANDSAT TM5 imagery and LiDAR elevation data (table 1). Using these preliminary 2010 LCRE data, we have preliminarily identified 26 classes in Reach F (fig. 7). Among the vegetated classes, in addition to agriculture, aquatic beds and tree farms, 4 are upland and 12 are wetland classes. Water, rock, mud, sand, urban, and "other" classes (for example, bare ground and developed open space) constitute the un-vegetated classes. Among the vegetation classes are: (1) five tidal wetland classes (coniferous, deciduous, mixed forest, scrub-shrub, and herbaceous); and (2) the equivalent classes for both non-tidal and upland areas of the Reach F.

Discussion

General and Unique Applicability to Estuarine Classification Needs

We have developed the Columbia River Estuary Ecosystem Classification to address the same need for estuaries as described by Poole (2002) for dynamic, patchy, and strongly hierarchical river and stream networks: "...a hierarchical patch dynamics perspective [that] can be used as a framework for visualizing interactions between structure and function..." While the landscape-scale relationships between structure and function in fluvial ecosystems is increasingly understood (Mertes, 2002; Poole, 2002; Poole and others, 2002; Wiens, 2002; Stanford and others, 2005; Strayer and others, 2006), similar research is lacking in large, freshwater dominated estuaries and deltas. The Classification offers a template for more detailed, process-based tests of those structure-function relationships. Moreover, the Classification is based primarily on spatially explicit datasets, which are key resources for interpreting estuarine hydrology, geomorphology, and ecosystem structure (Gilvear and others, 2004; Hume and others, 2007). Additionally, as spatial datasets are collected over time, the Classification provides a framework for assessments of ecosystem change and examinations of structure and function over multiple time scales and with respect to multiple stressors (for example, climate conditions, land use, and large-scale geologic events).

As tidal freshwater ecosystems cannot be disassociated from saline ecosystems in estuaries, we propose that pursuing fundamentally different approaches to ecosystem classification in fluvial and estuarine systems misses potentially strong controlling factors of rivers and their watersheds on estuarine structure and function (Hume and others, 2007). As illustrated by the challenges at developing a common definition and understanding of the term "transitional waters" (McLusky and Elliott, 2007) in the European Communities' Water Framework Directive (European Communities, 2000), estuaries encompass a continuum near coastal ocean, estuarine, and fluvial environments. At a minimum, the Classification addresses the identified need for the "division of transitional water system into management units that can usefully inform the decision-making process" (Ferreira and others, 2006) as well as effective management and rehabilitation.

Utility and Application to Estuarine Science, Monitoring, Restoration and Management

The Classification assesses biophysical datasets to develop a hierarchical representation of estuarine ecosystems where the ecosystem units at finer spatial scales (Level 3–Hydrogeomorphic Reach to Level 5–Geomorphic Catena) have particular geomorphic and hydrologic relevance to estuarine resource management issues. The Classification provides a visualization tool for examining the diversity and spatial distribution of ecosystem units across multiple spatial scales. Because the Classification also will be applicable to other estuarine systems where the necessary data (table 1) are available (Hume and others, 2007), it will help to promote and facilitate research, monitoring, restoration/preservation, and management efforts at regional and other spatial scales.

Research

The Classification provides a viable template that scientists can apply to stratify large, dynamic systems like the Columbia River estuary into manageable, discrete units for intensive and/or spatially extensive study and formulation of testable hypotheses. The structure of the Classification and the inherent integration of data necessary to formulate the hierarchical levels will allow scientists to assess landscape-level changes in the estuary (see section, "Change Analyses"). Using the Classification as a template and data resource, many possibilities exist to conduct research assessing the relationships between landscape-scale metrics and population dynamics and viability of important fish and wildlife species in estuarine ecosystems (Turner, 2005). Although the current lack of high-resolution data prevents us from final delineation of all hierarchical levels in the Classification, the rapid advancement of the technologies needed to efficiently collect the necessary data suggest that the data will become less expensive to collect and increase in widespread availability over time.

Alternatively, research may focus on relating physical conditions and biota within specific ecosystem complexes and/or geomorphic catenae. This type of research may yield information on those ecosystems that support vegetation, fish, and wildlife assemblages of concern or contribute substantial fluxes of organic matter, nutrients, and other basal food web resources to estuarine ecosystems. In this respect, an important validation of the Classification will be to test whether Geomorphic Catena can serve as identifiable habitats of estuarine fish and wildlife species of concern in the Columbia River estuary, such as juvenile Pacific salmon as they migrate through the estuary. Because of the threatened and endangered status among many of the Columbia River's salmon populations, understanding the association between prevalent controlling factors such as hydrology (including anthropogenic flow regulation) and the structure and evolution of habitat features (primarily at the geomorphic catena level) required by juvenile salmon is a critical step to enhancing habitat diversity for salmon recovery (Bottom and others, 2005).

Change Analyses

In addition to spatial analyses within and between systems, a standardized method for delineating ecosystems provides a framework for temporal analyses of ecosystem change. These analyses are particularly relevant for dynamic estuarine systems where the distribution, area, and maturity of different ecosystems vary in response to interacting controlling factors such river inflow, tidal variation, sediment inputs, and management actions such as regulation of river discharge and constructions of dikes and levees. Because the Classification's method for ecosystem delineation is not apt to change substantially over time, monitoring agencies could apply the Classification to datasets as they become available in order to identify and assess changes in ecosystem types. With this information, monitoring entities could examine effects of management actions (for example, discharge regulation, diking, dredging, and restoration actions) and climate change on estuarine ecosystems and communities over time.

As an example, we have applied the Classification's geospatial processing procedures for Level 6—Primary Cover Class to the 1866–1901 United States Coast and Geodetic Survey (USCGS) "t-sheet" topographic surveys for Reach F and compared the symbology for distinguishable land cover vegetation classes against our current draft of Level 6–Primary Cover Class (fig. 7) for a segment of the flood plain (fig. 8). This comparison suggests that while the basic structure of ecosystem complexes within the original survey area has not changed significantly over the past about 100 years, landscape metrics derived for five comparable vegetation cover classes (embedded in geomorphic catenae) quantify changes in complex dimensions and shapes and may indicate changes in their function in the estuary. Overall, the total area of floodplain forest and wetland forest ecosystems decreased significantly between 1866–1901 and 2010, less prominent floodplain scrub-shrub and wetland herbaceous ecosystems increased somewhat, and wetland scrub-shrub was a minor component historically and currently. In contrast, several metrics of patch complexity (total edge, shape, and perimeter:area ratio) have uniformly increased from historical to current conditions, especially wetland herbaceous (total edge and shape) and wetland forest (perimeter:area ratio). From a landscape ecology perspective, these trends could be associated with patch fragmentation, which has complex implications for changes in ecosystem function. However, how these changes may relate to altered hydrogeomorphic processes and resulting shifts in geomorphic catenae requires considerably more analysis.

Monitoring

The Classification's standardized delineation of ecosystem components is an effective communication tool for entities collecting, analyzing and sharing monitoring datasets within and between estuaries. The Classification also can be used to design robust status and trend monitoring efforts. Habitat and fish monitoring programs within the Columbia Basin inform various management needs; including the requirements of Biological Opinions on the operation of the Federal Columbia River Power System, tracking the recovery of species listed under the Endangered Species Act, and addressing the needs of the Northwest Power and Conservation Council's Fish and Wildlife Program. Like the Columbia River estuary, the management of other estuarine systems typically is multi-jurisdictional in nature. As an example, the Columbia River estuary (1) is within the jurisdiction of two States (Oregon and Washington) and numerous Federal, Tribal, watershed council, county, and municipal entities; (2) is the focus of ongoing recovery efforts for four ESA listed anadromous salmonid species (coho, chum, Chinook, and steelhead) and bull trout, and (3) has diverse land use and increasing human population pressures. Although there is a growing need for an integrated approach to long-term status and trend monitoring programs (Pacific Northwest Aquatic Monitoring Partnership , 2009), the Classification can help facilitate the evaluation of the status and trends of ecosystem attributes at multiple scales that accommodate the multi-jurisdictional monitoring needs of estuarine systems. Furthermore, if the resources were available to support a comprehensive status and trend monitoring program of indicators that are ecologically significant to listed salmonids in the Columbia River estuary, the hierarchical levels of the Classification could be used as attribute data in status and trend monitoring designs, such as a rotational split-panel design (Johnson and others, 2008; see: *http://www.pnl.gov/main/publications/external/technical_reports/PNNL-17300.pdf*; Appendix B) and/or to weight site selection using a Generalized Random-Tessellation Stratified (GRTS) framework (Larsen and others, 2008). Using the Classification to inform a master sample could enable management entities to stratify sampling locations by specific ecosystem complex or geomorphic catena classes relevant to culturally and economically important fish and wildlife species.

The Classification is intended to support metadata analyses of abiotic and biotic conditions among different estuary systems. Such analyses would provide a heuristic exercise for testing our scientific understanding of these systems and enable assessments of estuarine conditions at regional and international levels, such as among the large estuaries of western North America (including San Francisco Bay and Delta, Columbia River, Puget Sound, and the Fraser River), which have (or did historically have) extensive tidal freshwater ecosystems. Hydrographic reaches based on seasonal water and sediment quality attributes have been developed for the San Francisco estuary (San Francisco Estuary Institute , 2005) in a similar manner to the Classification's hydrogeomorphic reaches. Analyses among these systems could explore topics including the capacity of Pacific Rim estuaries to sustain wild salmonid populations and interactions among tidal vegetation assemblages and rising sea levels.

Restoration and Preservation Planning

We also consider the Classification useful for ecosystem restoration and preservation applications where the goal is to restore and protect functional ecosystems. With directed research, the Classification could be used as a tool in support of restoration planning efforts at different spatial scales. At the project level, Classification datasets provide the basis for assessments of the complexity and diversity of complexes and/or catenae using landscape ecology metrics. Initial actions could then focus on restoring and protecting sites with high ecosystem complexity and diversity. At larger scales, Classification datasets in conjunction with ecosystem stressor datasets (for example, road densities, urban and industrial locations, and sites with known toxic contamination, Evans and others, 2006) can be used to determine the proximity of candidate restoration sites to stressors of concern and account for potential confounding impacts at project sites. At the estuary-wide scale, restoration implementers could incorporate information on complexes and catenae that support fishes and wildlife of concern (as these data become available) in order to select projects that establish refuge habitats, or "stepping stones," along estuarine and tidal-freshwater corridors. These habitats would facilitate the movement of organisms between less hospitable ecosystems and throughout estuarine systems.

Management

Relative to estuarine resource management, the Classification provides a system-wide context for linking ecosystem spatial and temporal dynamics and management actions. In particular, the Classification's delineation methods reflect a process-based approach where geomorphic and hydrologic processes act at multiple time scales and vary longitudinally and laterally throughout the estuary of focus. These processes emphasize ecosystem formation and change over time instead of a static distribution of ecosystems. Furthermore, Classification datasets reflect a "snap shot" of conditions when ancillary datasets were collected (fig. 8). As research quantifies key geomorphic and hydrologic drivers of ecosystem condition in estuaries, agencies can use this information to implement management actions (such as releases of river discharges that form and maintain ecosystems; removal or setbacks of dikes to improve connections between mainstem and off-channel ecosystems) that support dynamic estuarine systems. These types of actions are apt to support recovery efforts for fish and wildlife populations of concern that are adapted to variable estuarine conditions (for example pertaining to salmonids, Bottom and others, 2005).

We acknowledge that the context of the Classification is extensively embedded in the management issues surrounding the Columbia River estuary. Since completion of the Estuary Partnership's Comprehensive Conservation and Management Plan (LCR-CCMP) (Lower Columbia River Estuary Program, 1999), organization of monitoring, management and education has depended to a large degree on understanding the distribution and status of ecosystems and biota-specific habitats. Included among 43 discrete actions recommended in the LCR-CCMP plan are those that would: (a) "inventory and prioritize habitat types and attributes needing protection and conservation"; (b) "identify habitats and environmentally sensitive lands that should not be altered"; (c) "protect, conserve and enhance identified habitats, particularly wetlands, on the mainstem of the lower Columbia River"; and (d) "adopt and implement consistent wetland, riparian, and instream habitat protection standards to increase the quality and quantity of habitat to protect aquatic species." Although considerable information was available for the lower about 75 km of estuary (Thomas, 1983; see also dedicated issue of *Progress in Oceanography*, 1990, 24(1-4), L.F. Small, guest ed.), the lack of a clear accounting of the types and spatial organization of the diverse ecosystems that composed the about 230 km of the lower River and estuary was cited as a critical limitation in implementing the recommended actions. Commensurate with this information gap was the lack of an ecosystem classification that would allow scientifically-based delineation of habitats at a variety of scales required for different monitoring, planning and management needs.

Constraints on Data Adequacy and Application of the Classification to the Entire Columbia River Estuary

Current constraints on application and validation of all levels of the Classification to the entire Columbia River estuary include incomplete and outdated bathymetric datasets for the estuary, LiDAR gaps for low elevation tidally influenced features like mudflats, and low accuracy for wetland features in available land-cover datasets (for example, LANDSAT 7 from 2000). Of these datasets, the bathymetry is the least consistent due to the dynamic nature of the Columbia River riverbed and differences in spatial resolution of the original surveys and propagation of errors associated with combining surveys from a 7-year period.

The completion of the lower three levels of the Classification (Ecosystem Complex, Geomorphic Catena, and Primary Cover Class) is anticipated to be complete by late 2011 in cooperation with the Estuary Partnership. GIS data layers, metadata, and final report will be made available to regional partners by the Estuary Partnership. Combined, these surveys are anticipated to provide a consistent bathymetric dataset for the lower and middle estuary, enabling completion of Level 4–Ecosystem complexes. Training and field checking for a new classified land-cover dataset are scheduled for 2010–11 and subsequent processing in winter 2011 under coordination by LCREP. This new land-cover dataset and the bathymetry data will support delineation of Level 5–Geomorphic Catena and Level 6–Primary Cover Class for the entire estuary.

Validation Needs

At this time, the Classification has not been formally validated with field data. Upon completion of all Classification levels for the entire estuary, a statistically rigorous, field-based validation of the Classification should be conducted to test for the appropriateness of the ecosystem complex and geomorphic catena levels and the classes and subdivisions within each level.

Summary and Recommendations

This description of the concept and framework for the Columbia River Estuarine Ecosystem Classification also explains the rationale for advancing an ecosystem process-based classification that captures the variation and mechanisms in formative processes that shape estuarine ecosystems along the continuum from the head of tide to the ocean entrance. This Classification was developed to reflect the complex physiographic setting and geologic history of the Columbia River estuary and dynamic processes reworking that landscape in a domain of significant tidal and riverine discharge modifications. As such, this Classification may be more complex than classifications developed for estuaries in less dynamic settings. However, we suggest that the scope and scale of this classification would serve as a robust starting framework for analysis of other estuarine systems.

Based on our experience developing the Classification template and recognition that the three most complex levels have yet to be fully delineated for the Columbia River estuary, we recognize these persistent science and information gaps:

1. Considerably more scientific investigations are needed to understand the processes and associated rates of change that structure the estuarine ecosystem, especially in tidal freshwater reaches where tidal influence generally is mediated by freshwater discharge.

2. More effort should be expended to compare estuarine classification systems that are similarly based on hydrogeomorphic controlling factors, such that classifications for different regions and types of estuaries can at least be cross-walked and ecosystem composition and structure compared.

3. Considerable more attention needs to be given to the geologic and tectonic processes that shaped estuaries as we know them, and particularly those processes that are still active, even if on very low frequency (but potentially very high magnitude) time scales. The prospects of sea-level rise and other manifestations of climate change makes this process-based understanding of large, landscape-scale influences on estuarine structure even more important.

4. Management applications of ecosystem classifications need to be tested with regional experts. The practicality and feasibility of monitoring large, dynamic estuaries based on a classification (such as proposed here) may have to balance statistical rigor and ecological significance.

Acknowledgments

Under the coordination of the Lower Columbia River Estuary Partnership, and through the support of the Bonneville Power Administration (BPA) and the U.S. Geological Survey (USGS), we have since 2004 been formulating an estuarine ecosystem classification that addresses these needs for the Columbia River and other comparable, large-river flood-plain estuaries. The Estuary Partnership has provided substantial assistance in coordinating acquisition of new bathymetric, land-cover and other critical datasets, as well as facilitating review of and refinements to the Classification throughout its development; we are particularly indebted to Keith Marcoe, Estuary Partnership GIS and Data Management Specialist, for facilitating acquisition and classification of new land cover/land use data for the estuary and for reviewing the emerging Ecosystem Complex and Geomorphic Catena classes. Support for preparing this document was provided by the Estuary Partnership while support for publication of this document was provided by a USGS Assistance Award (#05HQAG0096). Valuable technical support was provided by James Hatten and Tom Batt (USGS) who compiled a single bathymetric dataset of points from numerous data sources.

References Cited

Allee, R.J., Dethier, M., Brown, D., Deegan, L., Ford, G.R., Hourigan, T.R., Maragos, J., Schoch, C., Sealey, K., Twilley, R., Weinstein, M.P., and Yoklavich, M., 2000, Marine and Estuarine Ecosystem and Habitat Classification: National Oceanic and Atmospheric Administration, Technical Memorandum NMFS-F/SPO-43.

Atwater, B.F., 1987, Status of glacial Lake Columbia during the last floods from glacial Lake Missoula:Quaternary Research, v. 27, p. 182-201.

Atwater, B.F. (compiler), 1994, Geology of liquefaction features about 300 years old along the lower Columbia River at Marsh, Brush, Price, Hunting, and Wallace Islands, Oregon and Washington: U.S. Geological Survey Open-File Report 94-209.

Atwater, B.F., 2005, The orphan Tsunami of 1700—Japanese clues to a parent earthquake in North America: U.S. Geological Survey Professional Paper 1707, 133 p.

Atwater, B.F., and Hemphill-Haley, E., 1997, Recurrence intervals for great earthquakes of the past 3500 years at northeastern Willapa Bay, Washington: U.S. Geological Survey Professional Paper 1576, 108 p.

Bailey, R.G., 1983, Delineation of ecosystem regions: Environmental Management, v. 7, p. 365-373.

Bailey, R.G., 1987, Suggested hierarchy of criteria for multi-scale ecosystem mapping: Landscape and Urban Planning, v. 14, p. 313-319.

Bailey, R.G., 1995, Ecoregions of the Oceans: U.S. Dept of Agriculture, Forest Service, Washington, D.C.

Bailey, R.G., 1996, Ecosystem Geography: Springer, New York, 204 p.

Bailey, R.G., Avers, P.E., King, T., and McNab, W.H., 1994, Ecoregions and Subregions of the United States: U.S. Department of Agriculture Forest Service, Washington, DC.

Baross, J.A., Crump B., and Simenstad, C.A., 1994, Elevated microbial loop activities in the Columbia River estuarine turbidity maxima, *in* Dyer, K., and Orth, B., eds., Changing Particle Flux in Estuaries: Implications from Science to Management (ECSA22/ERF Symposium, Plymouth, September 1992), Olsen and Olsen Press, Fredensborg, p. 459-464.

Bayley, P.B., 1995, Understanding large river-floodplain ecosystems: Ecology of Large Rivers, BioScience, v. 45, p. 153-158.

Benda, L., Poff, N.L., Miller, D., Dunne, T., Reeves , G., Pess, G., and Pollock, M., 2004, The network dynamics hypothesis—how channel networks structure riverine habitats: BioScience, v. 54, p. 413–427.

Bottom, D.L., Simenstad, C.A., Burke, J., Baptista, A.M., Jay, D.A., Jones, K.K., Casillas, E., and Schiewe, M.H., 2005, Salmon at river's end: The role of the estuary in the decline and recovery of Columbia River salmon.: U.S. Department of Commerce, NOAA Technical Memorandum NMFS-NWFSC-68, 246 p., accessed July 5, 2011, at *http://www.nwfsc.noaa.gov/publications/displayallinfo.cfm?docmetadataid=6294.*

Bovee, K.D., 1982, A guide to stream habitat analysis using the instream flow incremental methodology: U.S. Fish and Wildlife Service FWS/OBS-82/26, 248 p.

Brown, B., 1993, A classification system of marine and estuarine habitats in Maine—an ecosystem approach to habitats: Maine Natural Areas Program, Department of Economic and Community Development, Augusta, Maine, 51 p.

Burgette, R.J., Weldon II, R.J., and, Schmidt, D.A., 2009, Interseismic uplift rates for western Oregon and along-strike variation in locking on the Cascadia subduction zone: Journal of Geophysical Research, v. 114, B01408, doi:10.1029/2008JB005679.

Clark, E.E., 1952, The Bridge of the Gods in Fact and Fancy: Oregon Historical Quarterly, v. 53, p. 29–38.

Clark, S.M., and Snyder, G.R., 1969, Timing and extent of flow reversal in the lower Columbia River: Limnology and Oceanography, v. 14, p. 960-965.

Colle, B.A., Mass, C.F., 2000, The 5–9 February 1996 flooding event over the Pacific Northwest—sensitivity studies and evaluation of the MM5 precipitation forecasts: American Meteorological Society, v. 128, p. 593-617.

Connor, D.W., 1997, Marine biotope classification for Britain and Ireland: Joint Nature Conservation Review, Peterborough, United Kingdom.

Cooke, R.U., and J. Doornkamp, 1990, Geomorphology in Environmental Management: Oxford, United Kingdom, Clarendon Press, 432 p.

Cowardin, W.M., Carter, V., Golet, F.C., and LaRoe, E.T., 1979, Classification of wetlands and deepwater habitats of the United States: U.S. Fish and Wildlife Service, FWS/OBS-79/31 GPO 024-010-00524-6,103 p.

Crump, B.C., and Baross, J.A., 1996, Particle-attached bacteria and heterotrophic plankton associated with the Columbia River estuarine turbidity maxima: Marine Ecology Progress Series, v. 138, p. 265-273.

Crump, B.C., Armbrust, E.V., and Baross, J.A., 1999, Phylogenetic analysis of particle-attached and free-living bacterial communities in the Columbia River, its estuary, and the adjacent coastal ocean: Applied and Environmental Microbiology, v. 65, p. 3192-3204.

Dalrymplem, R.W., Zaitlin, B.A., and Boyd, R., 1992, Estuarine facies models—conceptual basis and stratigraphic implications: Journal of Sedimentary Research, v. 62, p. 1130-1146.

Dana, J.W., 1849, Geology, [U.S. Exploring Expedition under C. Wilkes, U.S.N.] Philadelphia, C. Sherman, 756 p., 21 pls.

Dethier, M.N., 1990, A Marine and estuarine habitat classification system for Washington State: Olympia, Washington, Washington State Department of Natural Resources.

Dethier, M.N., 1992, Classifying marine and estuarine natural communities: An alternative to the Cowardin system: Journal of Natural Areas, v. 12, p. 90-100.

Dionne, J.C., 1963, Towards a more adequate definition of the St. Lawrence estuary: *Zeitschrift fuer Geomorphologie,* v. 7, p. 36-44.

Elliot, C., 2004, Tidal emergent plant communities, Russian Island, Columbia River estuary: University of Washington, Seattle, Washington, M.S. thesis, 87 p.

Elliott, M., and McLusky, D.S., 2002, The need for definitions in understanding estuaries: Estuarine, Coastal and Shelf Science, v. 55, p. 815-827.

European Communities, 2000, Directive 2000/60/ED of the European parliament and of the Council of 23 October 2000 establishing a framework for Community action in the field of water policy: Official Journal of the European Communities, v. 43, no. L327, 75 p.

Evans, N.R., Thom, R.M., Williams, G.D., Vavrinec, J., Sobocinski, K.L., Miller, L.M., Borde, A.B., Cullinan, V.I., Ward, J.A., May, C.W., and Allen, C., 2006, Lower Columbia River restoration prioritization framework: Pacific Northwest National Laboratory Report PNWD-3652, Richland, Washington, 73 p.

Evarts, R.C., 2004a, Geologic map of the Ridgefield 7.5' quadrangle, Washington: U.S. Geological Survey Scientific Investigations Map 2834, scale 1:24,000. (Also available at *http://pubs.usgs.gov/sim/2004/2844*).

Evarts, R.C., 2004b, Geologic map of the Saint Helens quadrangle, Clark and Cowlitz Counties, Washington: U.S. Geological Survey Scientific Investigations Map 2834, scale 1:24,000. (Also available at *http://pubs.usgs.gov/sim/2004/2834*.)

Evarts, R.C., 2004c, Geologic map of the Woodland quadrangle, Clark and Cowlitz Counties, Washington: U.S. Geological Survey Scientific Investigations Map 2827, scale 1:24,000. (Also available at *http://pubs.usgs.gov/sim/2004/2827*.)

Evarts, R.C., and O'Connor, J.E., 2008, Geologic map of the Camas quadrangle, Clark County, Washington, and Multnomah County, Oregon: U.S. Geological Survey Scientific Investigations Map 3017, scale 1:24,000, 31 p.

Evarts, R.C., O'Connor, J.E., Wells, R.E., and Madin, I.P., 2009, The Portland Basin—a (big) river runs through it: GSA Today, v. 19, doi: 10.1130/GSATG58A.1.

Fain, A.M.V., Jay, D.A., Wilson, D.J., Orton, P.M., and Baptista, A.M., 2001, Seasonal, monthly and tidal patterns of particulate matter dynamics in the Columbia River estuary: Estuaries, v. 24, p.770-786.

Fairbridge, R., 1980, The estuary—its definition and geodynamic cycle, *in* Olausson, E., and Cato, I., eds., Chemistry and Geochemistry of Estuaries: New York, John Wiley and Sons.

Fenneman, N.M., and Johnson, D.W., 1946, Physiographic divisions of the conterminous U.S.: U.S. Geological Survey Special Map Series, scale 1:7,000,000.

Ferreira, J.G., Nobre, A.M., Simas, T.C., Silva, M.C., Newton, A., Bricker, S.B., Wolff, W.J., Stacey, P.E., and Sequeira, A., 2006, A methodology for defining homogeneous water bodies in estuaries—application to the transitional systems of the EU Water Framework Directive: Estuarine, Coastal and Shelf Science, v. 66, p. 468-482.

Fox, D.S., Bell, S., Nehlsen, W., and Damron, J., 1984, The Columbia River estuary—Atlas of physical and biological characteristics: Columbia River Estuary Data Development Program, Astoria, Oregon, 89 p.

Frissell, C.A., Liss, W.J., Warren, C.E., and Hurley, M.D., 1986, A hierarchical framework for stream habitat classification—viewing streams in a watershed context: Environmental Management, v. 10, p. 199–214.

Fuhrer, G.J., Tanner, D.Q., Morace, J.L., McKenzie, S.W., and Skach, K.A., 1996, Water quality of the Lower Columbia River Basin–Analysis of current and historical water quality data through 1994: U.S. Geological Survey Water Resources Investigations Report 95-4294, 157 p. (Also available at *http://or.water.usgs.gov/pubs_dir/Pdf/columbia_bistate.pdf*.)

Garland, R.D., 2004, Modeling dewatered and subyearling fall Chinook salmon rearing areas below Bonneville Dam on the Columbia River: Portland State University, Portland, Oregon, M.S. Thesis.

Garono, R.J., Robinson, R., and Simenstad, C.A., 2003, Estuarine and tidal freshwater habitat cover types along the Lower Columbia River Estuary determined from Landsat 7 ETM+ Imagery: Lower Columbia River Estuary Partnership technical report, Portland, Oregon, 18 p.

Gates, E.B., 1994, The Holocene sedimentary framework of the lower Columbia River basin: Portland State University, Portland, Oregon, M.S. Thesis, 210 p.

Gelfenbaum, G., Sherwood, C.R., Peterson, C.D., Kaminsky, G.M., Buijsman, M., Twichell, D.C., Ruggiero, P., Gibbs, A.E., and Reed, C., 1999, The Columbia River littoral cell—a sediment budget overview, in Coastal Sediments '99, Long Island, NY, 1999, Proceedings: Long Island, NY, American Society of Civil Engineers, p. 1660-1675.

Gilvear, D., Tyler, A., and Davids, C., 2004, Detection of estuarine and tidal river hydromorphology using hyper-spectral and LiDAR data—Forth estuary, Scotland, Estuarine and Coastal Shelf Science, v. 61, p. 379-392.

Gonzalez, O.J., 1996, Formulating an ecosystem approach to environmental protection: Environmental Management, v. 20, p. 597-605.

Gore, J.A., and Shields, F.D., Jr., 1995, Can large rivers be restored?: Bioscience, v. 45, p. 142–152.

Haeni, F.P., 1983, Sediment deposition in the Columbia and lower Cowlitz Rivers, Washington-Oregon, caused by the May 18, 1980, eruption of Mount St. Helens: U.S. Geological Survey Circular 850-K, 21 p.

Haushild, W.L., Perkins, R.W., Stevens, H.H., Demspter, G.R., Jr., and Glenn, J.L., 1966, Radionuclide transport in the Pasco to Vancouver, Washington reach of the Columbia River, July 1962 to September 1963: U.S. Geological Survey Open-File Report, 188 p.

Hickey, B.M., 1998, Coastal oceanography of Western North America from the tip of Baja California to Vancouver Island, in Brink, K.H., and Robinson, A.R., eds., The Sea, v. 11, Chapter 12: Wiley and Sons, Inc., New York.

Hickson, R.E., and Rodolf, D., 1951, History of the Columbia River jetties, in Johnson, J.W., ed., Proceedings of First Conference on Coastal Engineering: Council on Wave Research, The Engineering Foundation, Berkeley, California, p. 293-298.

Hubbell, D.W., Laenen, J.M., and McKenzie, S.W., 1983, Characteristics of Columbia River sediment following the eruptions of Mount St. Helens on May 18, 1980: U.S. Geological Survey Circular 850-J, 21 p.

Hume, T.M., and Herdendorf, C.E., 1988, A geomorphic classification of estuaries and its application to coastal resource management—a New Zealand example: Ocean and Shoreline Management, v. 11, p. 249-274.

Hume, T.M., Snelder, T., Weatherhead, M., and Liefting, R., 2007, A controlling factor approach to estuary classification: Ocean and Coastal Management, v. 50, p. 905-929.

Jacobson, R.B., and Galat, D.L., 2006, Flow and form in rehabilitation of large-river ecosystems—an example from the Lower Missouri River: Geomorphology, v. 77, p. 249-269.

Jacobson, R.B., Blevins, D.W., and Bitner, C.J., 2009, Sediment regime constraints on river restoration – An example from the Lower Missouri River, in James, L.A., Rathburn, S.L., and Whittecar, G.R., eds., Management and restoration of fluvial systems with broad historical changes and human impacts: Denver, Colo., Geological Society of America Special Paper 451, p. 1-22.

Jay, D.A., Giese, B.S., and Sherwood, C.R., 1990, Energetics and sedimentary processes in the Columbia River Estuary: Progress in Oceanography, v. 25, p. 157-174.

Jay, D.A., and Musiak, J.D., 1994, Particle trapping in estuarine turbidity maxima: Journal of Geophysical Research, v. 99, p. 446-461.

Johnson, G.E., Diefenderfer, H.L., Ebberts, B.D., Tortorici, C., Yerxa, T., Leary, J., and Skalski, R.J., 2008, Research, monitoring, and evaluation for the Federal Columbia River Estuary Program. Pacific Northwest National Laboratories, Report 17300. 62 p. and appendices.

Jordan, G.F., 1962, Large submarine sand waves: Their orientation and form are influenced by some the same factors that shape desert sand dunes: Science, v. 136, p. 839-848.

Klijn, F., and Udo de Haes, H.A., 1994, A hierarchical approach to ecosystems and its implications for ecological land classification: Landscape Ecology, v. 9, p. 89-104.

Kukulka, T., and Jay, D.A., 2003a, Impacts of Columbia River discharge on salmonid habitat—1. A nonstationary fluvial tide model: Journal of Geophysical Research, v. 108, no. C9, 3294, doi:10.1029/2003JC001829, accessed July 5, 2011 at http://www.agu.org/journals/jc/jc0309/2003JC001829/.

Kukulka, T., and Jay, D.A., 2003b, Impacts of Columbia River discharge on salmonid habitat—2, changes in shallow-water habitat: Journal of Geophysical Research, v. 108, no. C9, 3294, doi:10.1029/2002JC001382.

Larsen, D.P., Olsen, A.R., and Stevens, Jr., D.S., 2008, Using a master sample to integrate stream monitoring programs: Journal of Agricultural, Biological, and Environmental Statistics, v. 13, p. 243-254.

Leopold, L.B., and Wolman, M.G., 1957, River channel patterns—braided, meandering, and straight: U.S. Government Printing Office, Washington, D.C.

Lower Columbia River Estuary Program (LCREP), 1999, Lower Columbia River Estuary Plan—Comprehensive Conservation and Management Plan. Lower Columbia River Estuary Program, 223 p.

Madden, C.J., and Grossman, D.H., 2004, A Framework for coastal/marine ecological classification standard: Prepared for the National Oceanic and Atmospheric Administration, Under Contract EA-133C-03-SE-0275, NatureServe, Arlington, Virginia.

Madley, K., 2002, Florida system for classification of habitats in estuarine and marine environments (SCHEME): Report to U.S. Environmental Protection Agency, Florida Fish and Wildlife Conservation Commissions Florida Marine Research Institute, FMRI File Cod 2277-00-02-F, 43 p.

Mantua, N.J., and Hare, S.R., Zhang, Y., Wallace, J.M., and Francis, R.C., 1997, A Pacific interdecadal climate oscillation with impacts on salmon production: Bulletin of the American Meteorological Society, v. 78, p. 1069-1079.

McGarigal, K., and Marks, B.J., 1995, FRAGSTATS: spatial pattern analysis program for quantifying landscape structure: General Technical Report PNW-GTR-351, USDA Forest Service, Pacific Northwest Research Station, Portland, Oregon.

McLusky, D.S., and Elliott, M., 2004, The Estuarine Ecosystem—ecology, threats, and management: Oxford, Oxford University Press, 214 p.

McLusky, D.S., and Elliott, M., 2007, Transitional waters—new approach, semantics or just muddying the waters?: Estuarine, Coastal and Shelf Science, v. 71, p. 359-363.

Mertes, L.A., 2002, Remote sensing of riverine landscapes: Freshwater Biology, v. 47, p. 799-816.

Morgan, C.A., Cordell, J.R., and Simenstad, C.A., 1997, Sink or swim? Copepod population maintenance in the Columbia River estuarine turbidity maxima region: Marine Biology, v. 129, p. 309-317.

Naik, P.K., and Jay, D.A., 2005, Estimation of Columbia River virgin flow—1879 to 1928: Hydrological Processes, v. 19, p. 1807-1824, doi:10.1002/hyp.5636, accessed July 5, 2011 at http://onlinelibrary.wiley.com/doi/10.1002/hyp.5636/abstract.

National Academy of Sciences (NAS), 1992, Water transfers in the west—efficiency, equity, and the environment: Committee on Western Water Management, National Research Council, Washington, D.C. 320 p.

Neal, V.T., 1972, Physical aspects of the Columbia River and its estuary, *in* Pruter, A.T., and Alverson, D.L., eds., The Columbia River estuary and adjacent ocean waters: University of Washington Press, Seattle, Washington, p. 19-40.

Obermeier, S.F., and Dickenson, S.E., 2000, Liquefaction evidence for the strength of ground motions resulting from late Holocene Cascadia subduction earthquakes, with emphasis on the event of 1700 A.D.: Bulletin of the Seismological Society of America, v. 90, p. 876-896.

O'Connor, J.E., 2004, The evolving landscape of the Columbia River Gorge—Lewis and Clark and cataclysms on the Columbia: Oregon Historical Quarterly, v. 105, p. 390-421.

O'Connor, J.E., and Burns, S.F., 2009, Columbia cataclysms and controversy—aspects of the geomorphology of the Columbia River Gorge, *in* O'Connor, J.E., Dorsey, R.J., and Madin, I.P., eds., Volcanoes to Vineyards: Geologic Field Trips through the Dynamic Landscape of the Pacific Northwest: Geological Society of America Field Guide, v. 15, p. 237–251.

O'Connor, J.E., Pierson, T.C., Turner, D., Atwater, B.B., and Pringle, P.T., 1996, An exceptionally large Columbia River flood between 500 and 600 years ago—breaching of the Bridge-of-the-Gods Landslide?: Geological Society of America Abstracts with Programs, v. 28, p. 97.

Omernik, J.M., 1987, Ecoregions of the conterminous United States: Annals of the Association of American Geographers 77, p. 118-125. (Datasets accessed July 5, 2011 at http://www.epa.gov/wed/pages/ecoregions/ecoregions.htm.)

Omernik, J.M., 1995, Ecoregions: A spatial framework for environmental management, *in* Davis, W.S., and Simon, T.P., eds., Biological assessment and criteria: Boca Raton, Florida, Lewis Publishers, Tools for Water Resource Planning and Decision Making, p. 49-62.

Omernik, J.M., and Bailey, R.G., 1997, Distinguishing between watersheds and ecoregions: Journal of the American Water Resources Institute, v. 33, p. 935-949.

O'Neill, R.V., DeAngelis, D.L., Waide, J.B., and Allen, T.F.H., 1986, A hierarchical concept of ecosystems: Princeton, New Jersey, Princeton University Press, 249 p.

Pacific County Historical Society and Museum, 2000, Columbia River chronology historic dates: Pacific County Historical Society and Museum searchable database, South Bend, Washington, accessed July 5, 2011 at *http://www.pacificcohistory.org/*.

Pacific Northwest Aquatic Monitoring Partnership (PNAMP), 2009, Integrating aquatic ecosystem and fish status and trend monitoring in the Lower Columbia River: overview: PNAMP Series 2009-006.

Perillo, G.M.E., 1995, Definition and geomorphologic classifications of estuaries, *in* Perillo, G.M.E., ed., Geomorphology and sedimentology of estuaries: Developments in Sedimentology, v. 53. p. 17-47.

Peterson, C.D., Gelfenbaum, G.R., Jol, H.M., Phipps, J.B., Reckendorf, F., Twichell, D.C., Vanderburg, S., and Woxell, L.L., 1999, Great earthquakes, abundant sand, and high wave energy in the Columbia Cell, USA, *in* Kraus, N.C., and McDougal, W.G., eds., Coastal Sediments '99, Proceedings, American Society of Civil Engineers, 4th International Symposium: American Society of Civil Engineers, v. 2, p. 1676-1691.

Peterson, C.D., and Madin, I.P., 1997, Coseismic liquefaction evidence in the central Cascadia margin, USA: Oregon Geology, v. 59, p. 51-74.

Poff, N.L., Allan, J.D., Bain, M.B., Karr, J.R., Prestegaard, K.L., Richter, B.D., Sparks, R.E., and Stromberg, J.C., 1997, The natural flow regime: BioScience, v. 47, p. 769-784.

Poole, G.C., 2002, Fluvial landscape ecology—addressing uniqueness within the river continuum: Freshwater Biology, v. 47, p. 641-660.

Poole, G.C., Stanford, J.A., Frissell, C.A., and Running, S.W., 2002, Three-dimensional mapping of geomorphic controls on flood-plain hydrology from aerial photos: Geomorphology, v. 48, p. 329-347.

Prahl, F.P., and Coble, P.G., 1994, Input and behavior of dissolved organic carbon in the Columbia River Estuary, in Dyer, K., and Orth, B., eds., Changing particle flux in estuaries: Implications from Science to Management (ECSA22/ERF Symposium, Plymouth, September 1992), Olsen & Olsen Press, Fredensborg, p. 451-457.

Prahl, F.G., Small, L.F., and Eversmeyer, B.C., 1997, Biogeochemical characterization of suspended particulate matter in the Columbia River estuary: Marine Ecology Progress Series, v. 160, p. 174-184.

Prahl, F.P., Small, L.F., Sullivan, B., Cordell, J., Simenstad, C.A., Crump, B.C., and Baross, J.A., 1998, Biogeochemical gradients in the lower Columbia River: Hydrobiologia, v. 361, p. 37-52.

Rapp, E.K., 2005, The Holocene stratigraphy of the Sandy River Delta, Oregon: Portland State University, Portland, Oregon, M.S. Thesis, 99 p.

Reed, D.J., and Donovan, J., 1994, The character and composition of the Columbia River estuarine turbidity maximum, in Dyer, K., and Orth, B., eds., Changing Particle Flux in Estuaries: Implications from Science to Management (ECSA22/ERF Symposium, Plymouth, September 1992), Olsen & Olsen Press, Fredensborg, p. 445-450.

Rice, S.P., Roy, A.G., and Rhoads, B.L., eds., 2008, River confluences, tributaries and the fluvial network: Chichester, England, John Wiley and Sons, Ltd, 456 p.

Ritter, D.F., 1967, Rates of denudation: Journal of Geological Education, v. 15, p. 154-159.

Ropelewski, C., and Halpert, M., 1986, North American precipitation and temperature patterns associated with the El Niño/Southern Oscillation (ENSO): Monthly Weather Review, v. 114, p. 2352-2362.

Rosgen, D.L., 1994, A classification of natural rivers: Catena v. 22, p. 169-199.

San Francisco Estuary Institute (SFEI), 2005, Regional monitoring program for trace substances—redesign process of the San Francisco estuary regional monitoring program for trace substances (RMP) status and trends monitoring component for water and sediment: San Francisco Estuary Institute, Oakland, California.

Sear, D.A., Newson, M.D., and Thorne, C.R., 2003, Guidebook of applied fluvial geomorphology: R&D Technical Report FD1914, DEFRA/Environment Agency, Flood Coast. Def. Research and Development Program, Flood Management Division, London, United Kingdom.

Schuchardt, B., and Schirmer, M., 1991, Phytoplankton maxima in the tidal freshwater reaches of two coastal plain estuaries: Estuarine, Coastal and Shelf Science, v. 32, p. 187-206.

Schuster, R.L., 1981, Effects of the eruptions on civil works and operations in the Pacific Northwest, in Lipman, P.W., and Mullineaux, D.R., eds., The 1980 Eruptions of Mount St. Helens, Washington: U.S. Geological Survey Professional Paper 1250. (Also available at http://pubs.er.usgs.gov/publication/pp1250.)

Sherwood, C.R., and Creager, J.S., 1990, Sedimentary geology of the Columbia River estuary: Progress in Oceanography, v. 25, p. 15-79.

Sherwood, C.R., Jay, D.A., Harvey, R.B., Hamilton, P., and Simenstad, C.A., 1990, Historical changes in the Columbia River estuary: Progress in Oceanography, v. 25, p. 299-357.

Schuchardt, B., Haesloop, U., and Schirmer, M., 1993, The tidal freshwater reach of the Weser estuary: riverine or estuarine?: Netherlands Journal of Aquatic Ecology, v. 27, p. 215-226.

Simenstad, C.A., Jay, D.A., and Sherwood, C.R., 1992, Impacts of watershed management on land-margin ecosystems—the Columbia River estuary as a case study, *in* Naiman, R.J., ed., Watershed management—balancing sustainability and environmental change: New York, Springer-Verlag, p. 266-306.

Simenstad, C.A., Morgan, C.A., Cordell, J.R., and Baross, J.A., 1994a, Flux, passive retention, and active residence of zooplankton in Columbia River estuarine turbidity maxima, *in* Dyer, K., and Orth, B., eds., Changing particle flux in estuaries—implications from science to management: (ECSA22/ERF Symposium, Plymouth, September 1992), Olsen & Olsen Press, Fredensborg, p. 473-482.

Simenstad, C.A., Reed, D.J., Jay, D.A., Baross, J.A., Prahl, F.G., and Small, L.F., 1994b, Land-margin ecosystem research in the Columbia River estuary: investigations of the couplings between physical and ecological processes within estuarine turbidity maxima, *in* Dyer, K., and Orth, B., eds., Changing particle flux in estuaries—implications from science to management (ECSA22/ERF Symposium, Plymouth, September 1992), Olsen & Olsen Press, Fredensborg, p. 437-444.

Simons, J., Ohm, M., Koomen, A., van Rooij, S., and Pakes, U., 2001, An approach for a vision for the Rhine-Meuse estuary based on ecotopes and ecological networks (poster): Ministry of Transport, Public Works, Water Management, Institute Inland Water Management and Waste Water Treatment (RIZA), Netherlands.

Small, L.F., and Morgan, S.R., 1994, Phytoplankton attributes in the turbidity maximum of the Columbia River estuary, USA, *in* Dyer, K., and Orth, B., eds., Changing particle flux in estuaries—implications from science to management (ECSA22/ERF Symposium, Plymouth, September 1992), Olsen & Olsen Press, Fredensborg, p. 465-472.

Sowa, S.P., Annis, G., Morey, M.E., and Diamond, D.D., 2007, A gap analysis and comprehensive conservation strategy for riverine ecosystems of Missouri, v. 77, p. 301-334.

Stanford, J.A., 1998, Rivers in the landscape—introduction to the special issue on riparian and groundwater ecology: Freshwater Biology, v. 40, p. 402-406.

Stanford, J.A., Lorang, M.S., and Hauer, F.R., 2005, The shifting habitat mosaic of river ecosystems: Verhandlungen Internationale Vereinigung für theoretische und angewandte Limnologie, v. 29, p. 123-139.

Strayer, D.L., Malcom, H.M., Bell, B.E., Carbotte, S.M., and Nitsche, F.O., 2006, Using geophysical information to define benthic habitats in a large river: Freshwater Biology, v. 51, p. 25-38.

Sundborg, A., 1983, Sedimentation problems in river basins: Nature and Resources, v. 19, p. 10-21.

Syvitski, J.P.M., Harvey, N., Wolanski, E., Burnett, W.C., Perillo, G.M.E., Gornitz, V., Bokuniewicz, H., Huettel, M., Moore, W.S., Saito, Y., Taniguchi, M., Hesp, P., Yim, W.W-S., Salisbury, J., Campbell, J., Snoussi, M., Haida, S., Arthurton, R., and Gao, S., 2005b, Dynamics of the coastal zone, *in* Crossland, C.J., Kremer, H.H., Lindeboom, H.J., Crossland, J.I.M., and Le Tissier, M.D.A., eds., Coastal Fluxes in the Anthropocene: Berlín, Springer-Verlag, p. 39-94.

Syvitski, J.P.M., Vörösmarty, C.J., Kettner, A.J., and Green, P., 2005a, Impact of humans on the flux of terrestrial sediment to the global coastal ocean: Science, v. 308, p. 376-380.

Takada, K., and Atwater, B.F., 2004, Evidence for liquefaction identified in peeled slices of Holocene deposits along the lower Columbia River, Washington: Bulletin of the Seismological Society of America, v. 94, p. 550-575.

Tiffan, K.F., Garland, R.D., and Rondorf, D.W., 2002, Quantifying flow-dependent changes in subyearling fall chinook salmon rearing habitat using two dimensional spatially explicit modeling: North American Journal of Fisheries Management, v. 22, p. 713-726.

Thomas, D.W., 1983, Changes in the Columbia River Estuary habitat types over the last century: Astoria, Oregon, Columbia River Data Development Program, 17 p.

Turner, M.G., 2005, Landscape ecology— What is the state of the science?: Annual Review of Ecology, Evolution, and Systematics, v. 36, p.319–44.

US Army Corps of Engineers (USACE), 1968, Flood profiles— Columbia River and tributaries, Washington and Oregon, below Bonneville Dam: US Army Engineer District Portland, OR, CL-03-116.

U.S. Army Corps of Engineers (USACE), 1968 (revised), Columbia River and tributaries Washington and Oregon below Bonneville Dam—flood profiles: U.S. Army Engineer District, Portland, drawing CL-03-116.

U.S. Army Corps of Engineers, North Pacific Division (USACE-NPD), 1984, Columbia River Basin: Portland, Oregon, U.S. Army Corps of Engineers, Master Water Control Manual.

van der Molen, D.T., Geilen, N., Backx, J.J.G.M., Jansen, B.J.M., and Wolfert, H.P., 2003, Water ecotope classification for integrated water management in the Netherlands: European Water Association (EWA), European Water Management Online.

Vogel, M.S., 2005, Quaternary geology of the lower Lewis River valley, Washington—Influence of volcanogenic sedimentation following Mount St. Helens Eruptions: Pullman, Washington, Washington State University, M.S. Thesis, 65 p.

Vorosmarty, C. J., Green, P., Salisbury, J., and Lammers, R., 2000, Global water resources—vulnerability from climate change and population growth: Science, v. 289, p. 284–288.

Ward, J.V., Tockner, K., Arscott, D.D., and Claret, C., 2002, Riverine landscape diversity: Freshwater Biology, v. 47, p. 517-539.

Weins, J.A., 2002. Riverine landscapes: taking landscape ecology into the water: Freshwater Biology, v. 47, p. 501-515.

Whetten, J.T., and Fullam, T.J., 1967, Columbia River bed forms: Proceedings of XII Congress of the International Association for Hydraulic Research, v. 1, p. 107-114.

Whetten, J.T., Kelley, J.C., and Hanson, L.G., 1969, Characteristics of Columbia River sediment and sediment transport: Journal of Sedimentary Petrology, v. 39, p. 1,149-1,166.

Wieland, R.G., 1993, Marine and estuarine habitat types and associated ecological communities of Mississippi Coast: Mississippi Department of Wildlife Fisheries and Parks, Mississippi Natural Heritage program, Mississippi Museum of Natural Science, 25 p.

Wolanski E., 2007, Estuarine Ecohydrology: Amsterdam, Elsevier, 157 p.

Woxell, L.K., 1998, Prehistoric beach accretion rates and long-term response to sediment depletion in the Columbia River littoral system, USA: Portland, Oregon, Portland State University, M.S. Thesis, 206 p.

Appendix A. Summary of location, geographic and geomorphic setting, major landforms, geologic content and history, characteristic geomorphic and hydrologic processes, and anthropogenic factors affecting key processes in eight Hydrogeomorphic Reach forming the Columbia River Estuary Ecosystem Classification.

Reach A

Reach B

Reach C

Reach D

Reach E

Reach F

Reach G

Reach H

Appendix A is a Microsoft© Excel file and can be downloaded at http://pubs.usgs.gov/of/2011/1228.

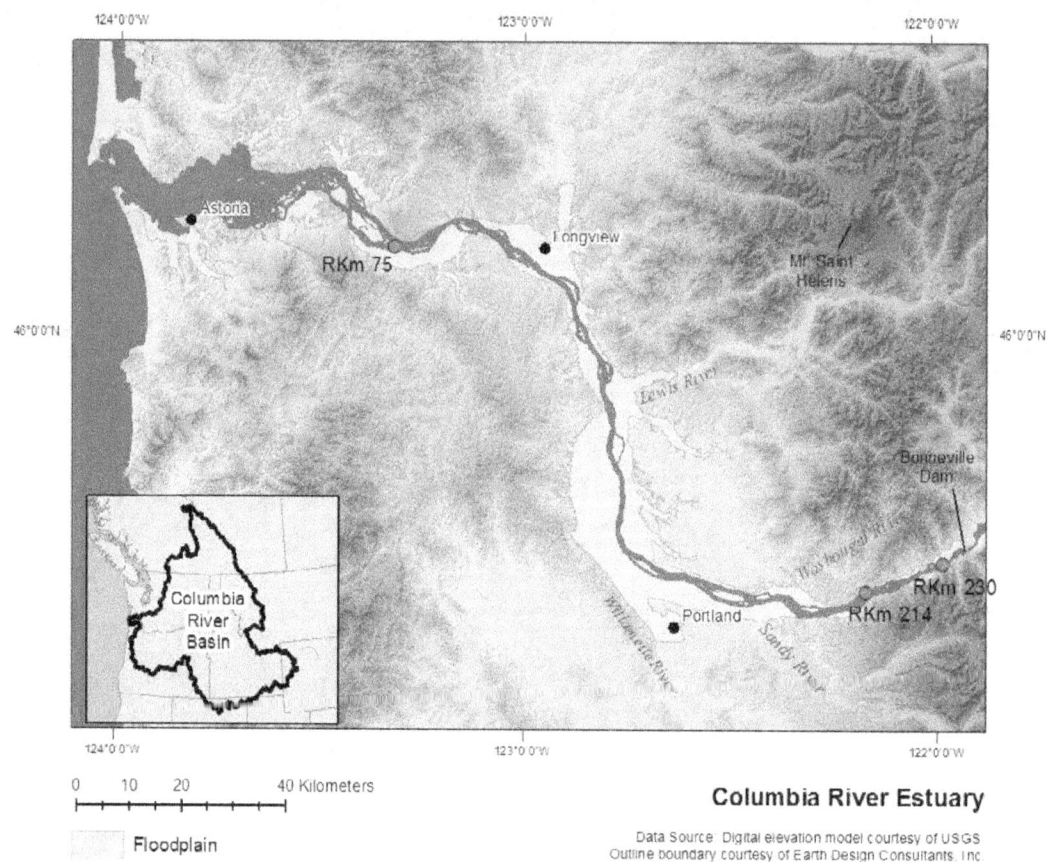

Figure 1. Basic physiographic setting and geographic extent of the Columbia River estuary as applied to the Columbia River Estuary Ecosystem Classification. Tentative flood-plain outline estimated by inclusion of all surfaces less than 18 m above the NAVD 1988.

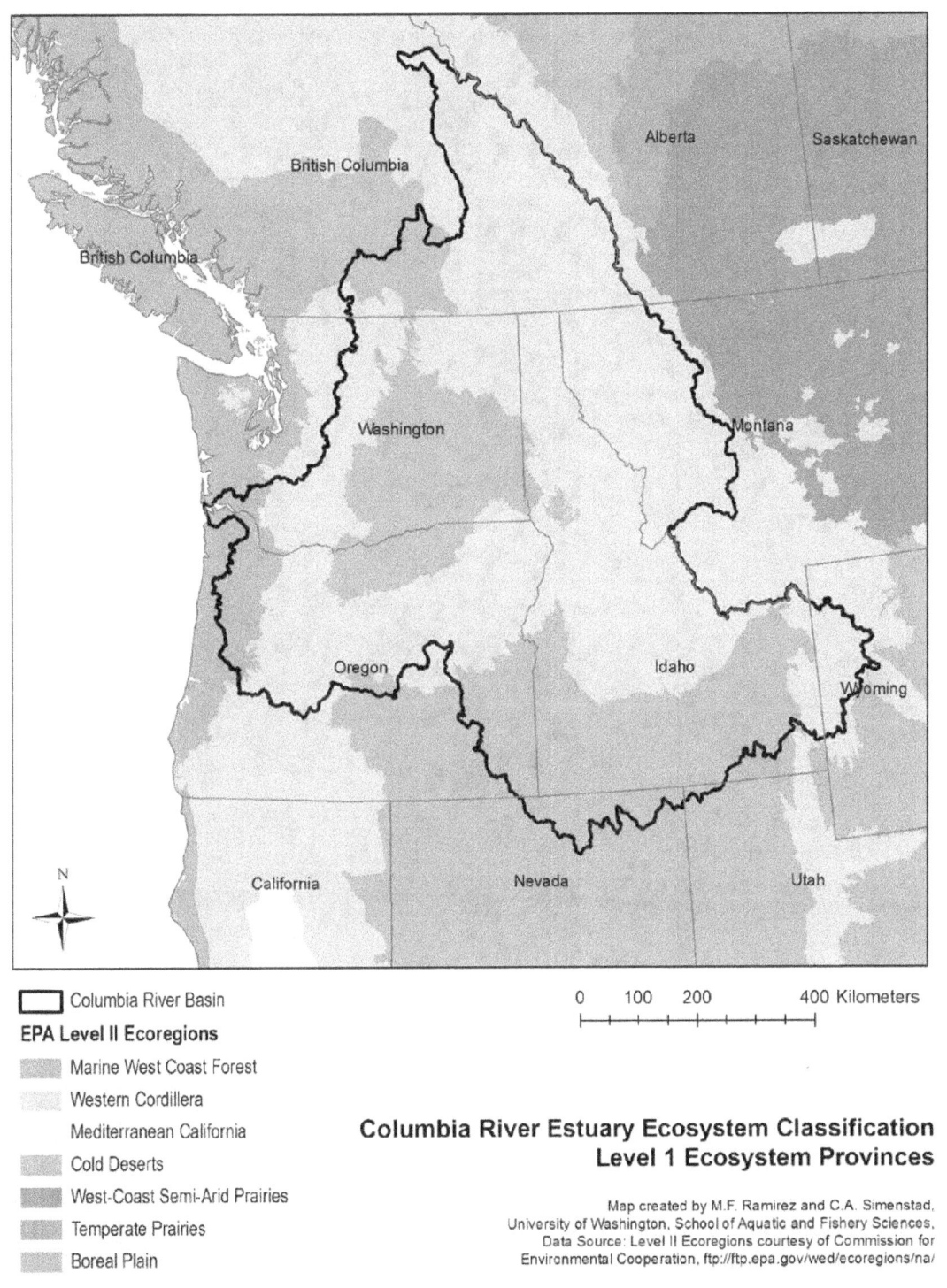

Columbia River Estuary Ecosystem Classification
Level 1 Ecosystem Provinces

Map created by M.F. Ramirez and C.A. Simenstad,
University of Washington, School of Aquatic and Fishery Sciences,
Data Source: Level II Ecoregions courtesy of Commission for
Environmental Cooperation, ftp://ftp.epa.gov/wed/ecoregions/na/

Figure 2. Classification Level 1-Ecoregion Provinces, adopting the EPA Ecoregion Level II classification.

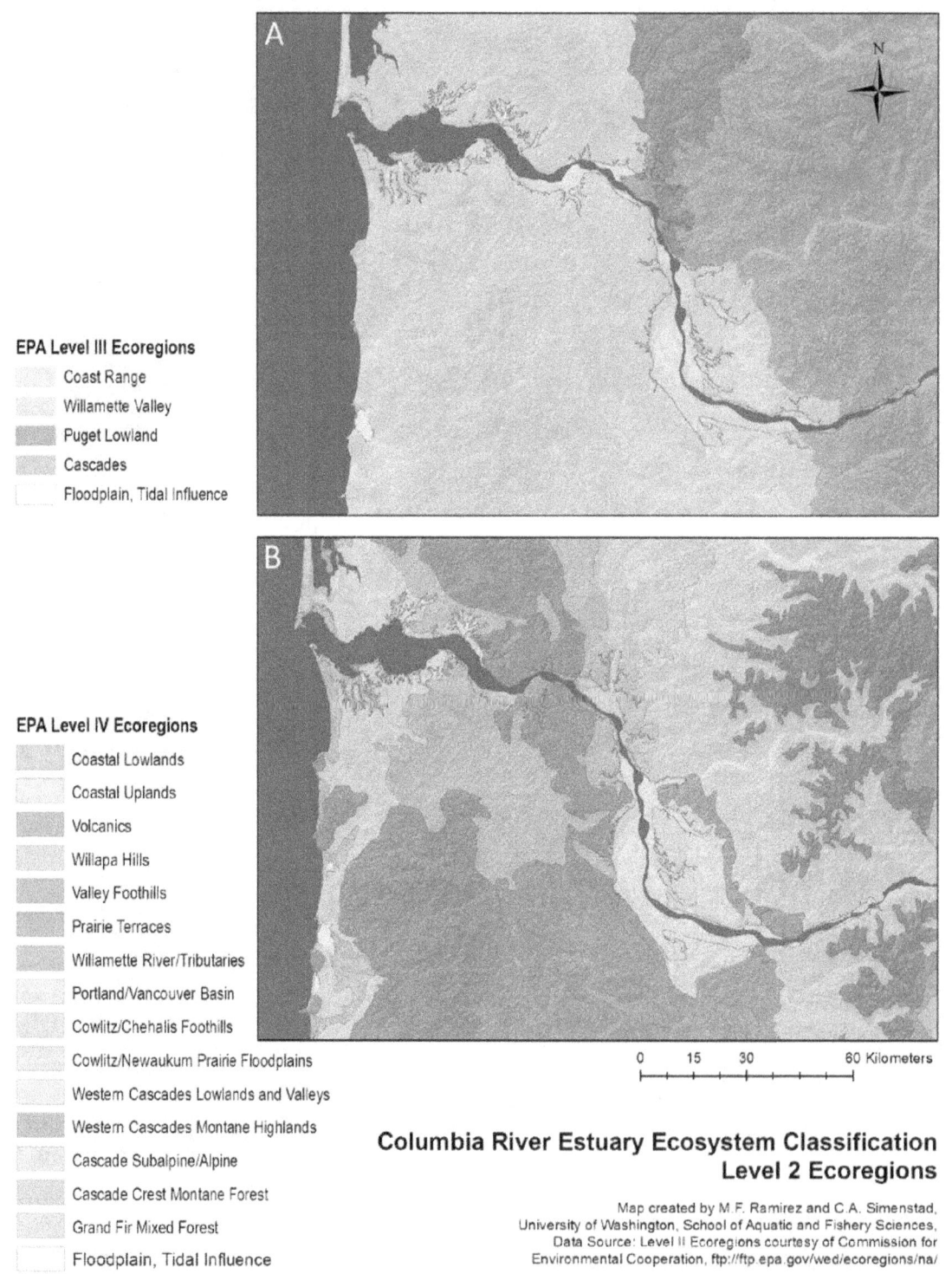

EPA Level III Ecoregions

- Coast Range
- Willamette Valley
- Puget Lowland
- Cascades
- Floodplain, Tidal Influence

EPA Level IV Ecoregions

- Coastal Lowlands
- Coastal Uplands
- Volcanics
- Willapa Hills
- Valley Foothills
- Prairie Terraces
- Willamette River/Tributaries
- Portland/Vancouver Basin
- Cowlitz/Chehalis Foothills
- Cowlitz/Newaukum Prairie Floodplains
- Western Cascades Lowlands and Valleys
- Western Cascades Montane Highlands
- Cascade Subalpine/Alpine
- Cascade Crest Montane Forest
- Grand Fir Mixed Forest
- Floodplain, Tidal Influence

0   15   30   60 Kilometers

Columbia River Estuary Ecosystem Classification
Level 2 Ecoregions

Map created by M. F. Ramirez and C.A. Simenstad,
University of Washington, School of Aquatic and Fishery Sciences,
Data Source: Level II Ecoregions courtesy of Commission for
Environmental Cooperation, ftp://ftp.epa.gov/wed/ecoregions/na/

Figure 3. Classification Level 2-Ecoregions based on the EPA Ecoregion classifications. A. EPA Ecoregion Level III classification. B EPA Ecoregion Level IV classification, which is nested in the Level III classes. Both maps show outline of tentative Columbia River estuary flood plain.

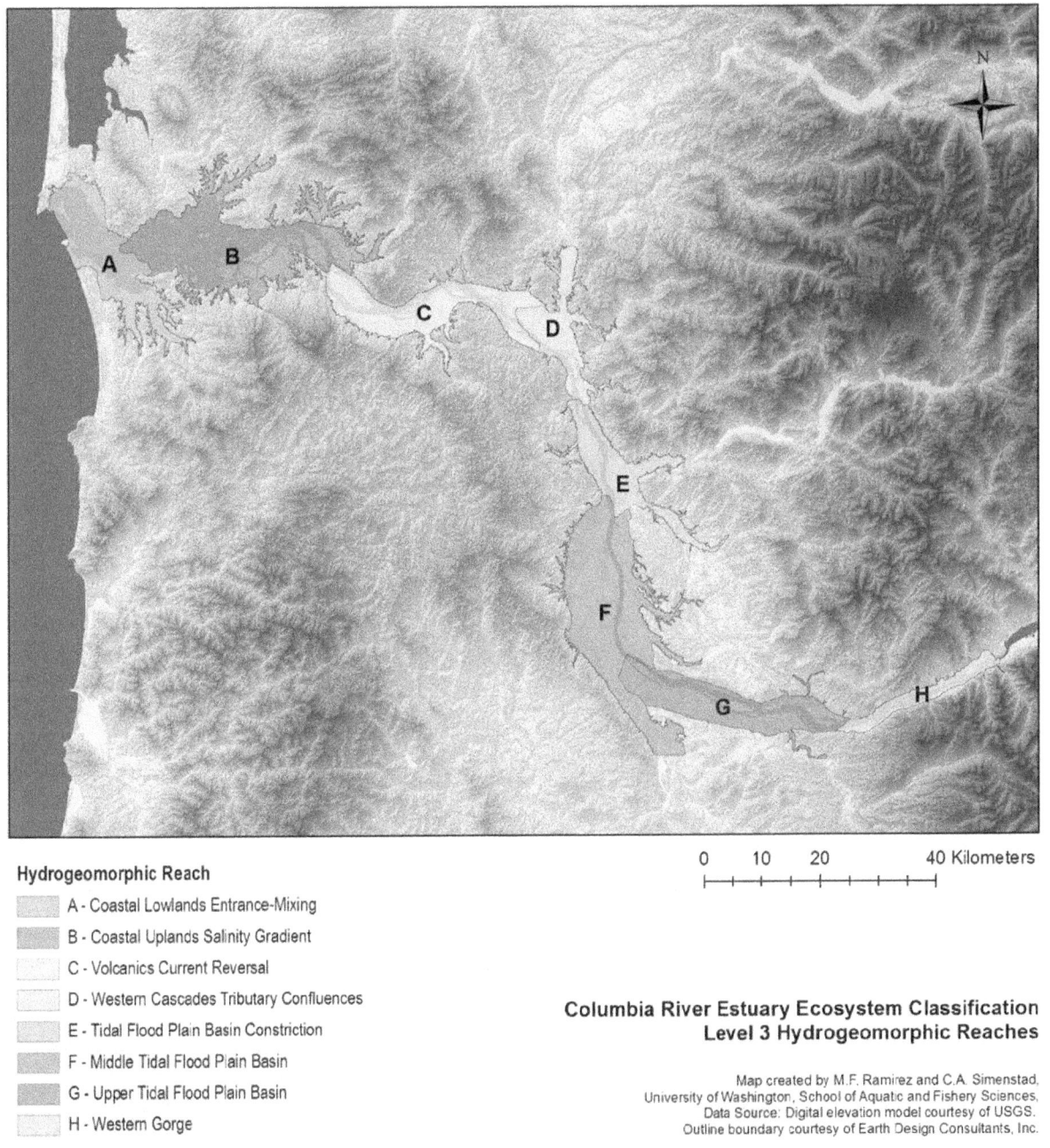

Figure 4. Classification Level 3-Hydrogeomorphic Reaches indicating where the eight reaches are delineated by subdividing and adjusting the borders of EPA Ecoregion IV classes (see Figure 3) according to hydrological and physiographic discontinuities (see Methods).

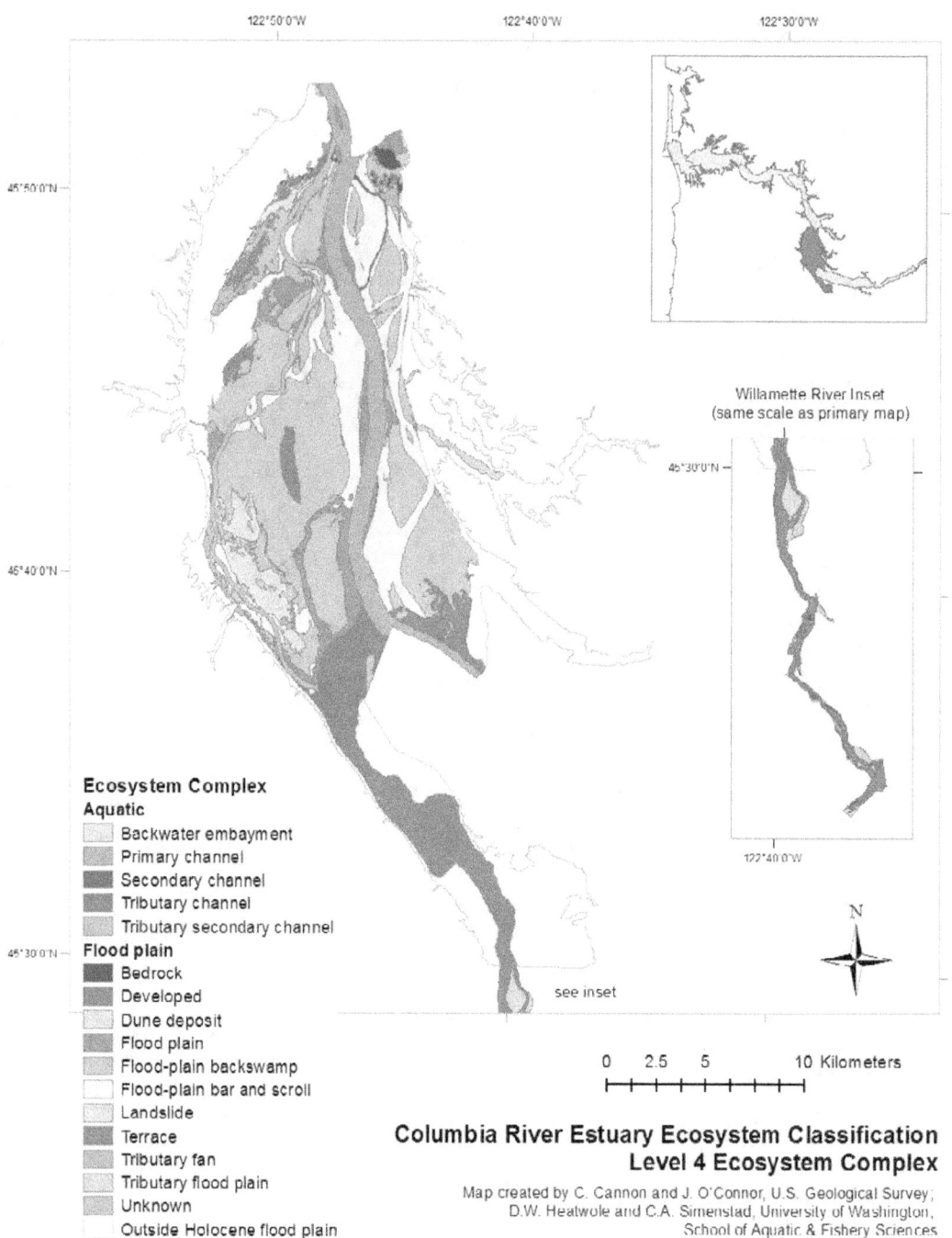

Ecosystem Complex
Aquatic
- Backwater embayment
- Primary channel
- Secondary channel
- Tributary channel
- Tributary secondary channel

Flood plain
- Bedrock
- Developed
- Dune deposit
- Flood plain
- Flood-plain backswamp
- Flood-plain bar and scroll
- Landslide
- Terrace
- Tributary fan
- Tributary flood plain
- Unknown
- Outside Holocene flood plain

**Columbia River Estuary Ecosystem Classification
Level 4 Ecosystem Complex**

Map created by C. Cannon and J. O'Connor, U.S. Geological Survey;
D.W. Heatwole and C.A. Simenstad, University of Washington,
School of Aquatic & Fishery Sciences

Figure 5. Classification Level 4-Ecosystem Complexes illustrated for Hydrogeomorphic Reach F (see fig. 4) based on delineating mainstem and distributary channels using current bathymetry data and analyses of flood plain geology and geomorphology (see Methods, table 1). Classified area reflects flood-plain boundary revised from initial elevation-based criteria (shown in inset and by area "outside Holocene flood plain" to only include area of Holocene fluvial deposition and modification as inferred from topographic, geological and soils maps.

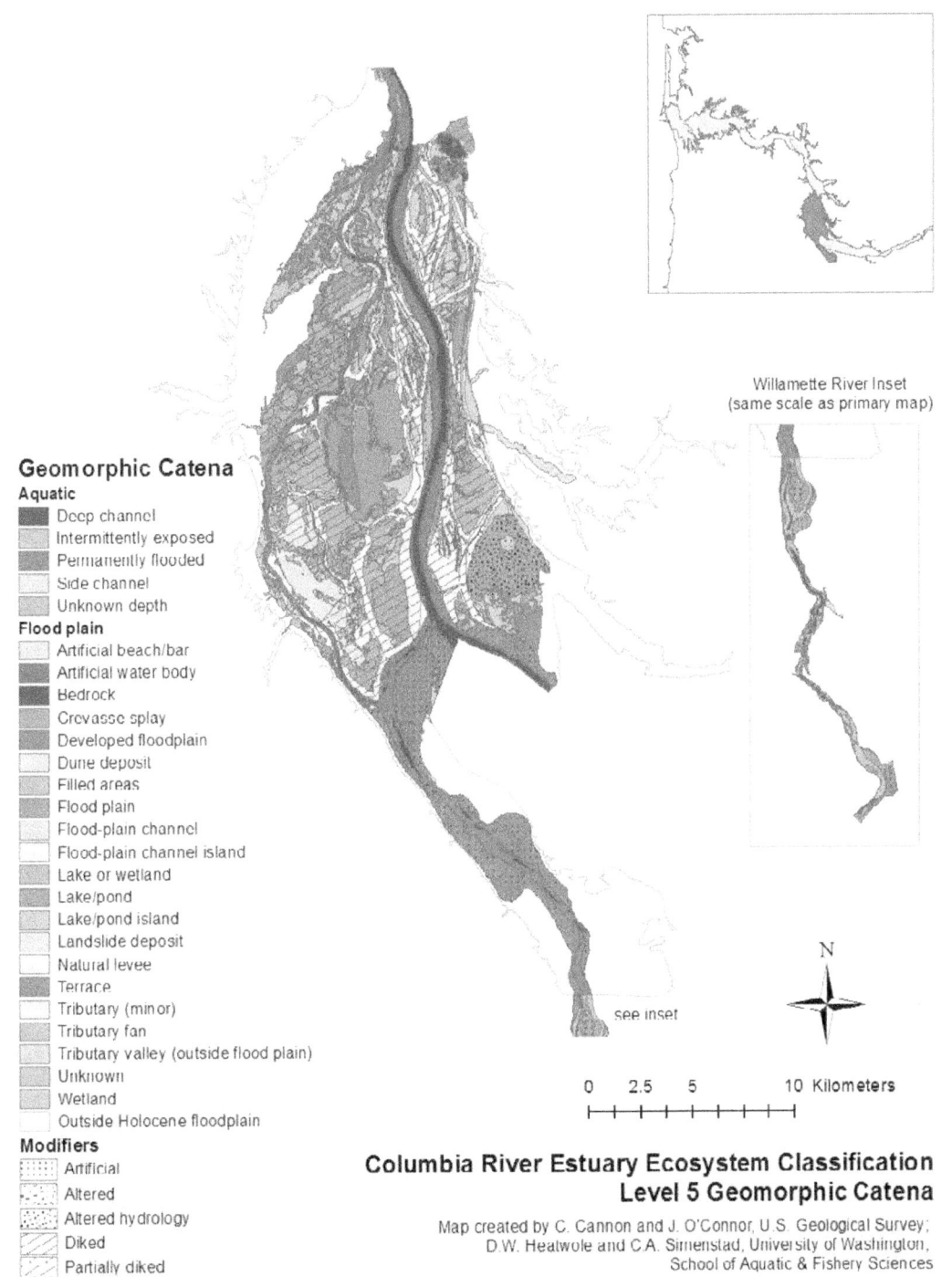

Geomorphic Catena

Aquatic
- Deep channel
- Intermittently exposed
- Permanently flooded
- Side channel
- Unknown depth

Flood plain
- Artificial beach/bar
- Artificial water body
- Bedrock
- Crevasse splay
- Developed floodplain
- Dune deposit
- Filled areas
- Flood plain
- Flood-plain channel
- Flood-plain channel island
- Lake or wetland
- Lake/pond
- Lake/pond island
- Landslide deposit
- Natural levee
- Terrace
- Tributary (minor)
- Tributary fan
- Tributary valley (outside flood plain)
- Unknown
- Wetland
- Outside Holocene floodplain

Modifiers
- Artificial
- Altered
- Altered hydrology
- Diked
- Partially diked

Willamette River Inset
(same scale as primary map)

N

0   2.5   5   10 Kilometers

Columbia River Estuary Ecosystem Classification
Level 5 Geomorphic Catena

Map created by C. Cannon and J. O'Connor, U.S. Geological Survey;
D.W. Heatwole and C.A. Simenstad, University of Washington,
School of Aquatic & Fishery Sciences

Figure 6. Classification Level 5-Geomorphic Catena illustrated for Hydrogeomorphic Reach F (see fig. 4). Classified area reflects flood-plain boundary revised from initial elevation-based criteria (shown in inset and by area "outside Holocene flood plain") to only include area of Holocene fluvial deposition and modification as inferred from topographic, geological, and soils maps.

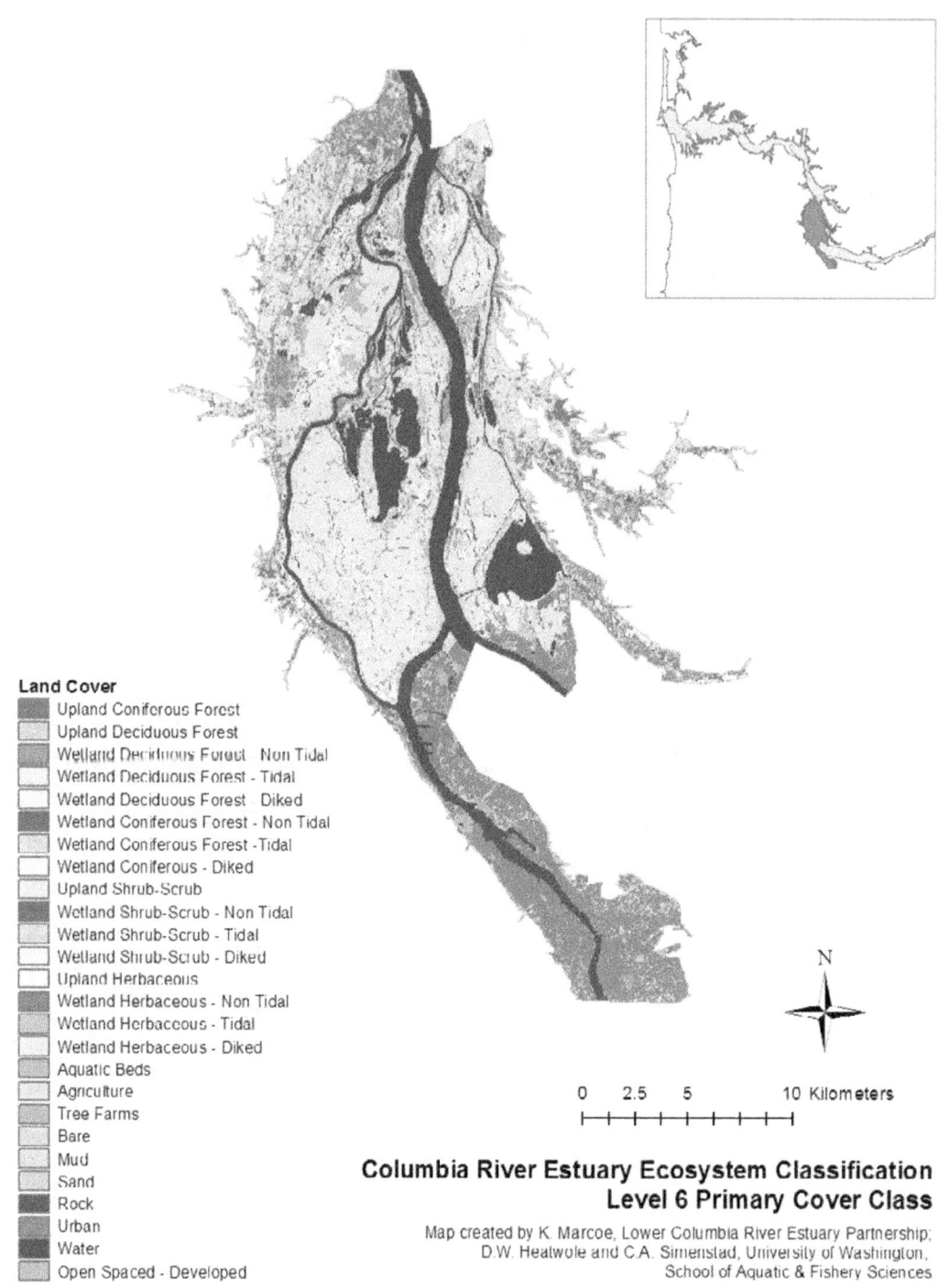

Land Cover

- Upland Coniferous Forest
- Upland Deciduous Forest
- Wetland Deciduous Forest - Non Tidal
- Wetland Deciduous Forest - Tidal
- Wetland Deciduous Forest - Diked
- Wetland Coniferous Forest - Non Tidal
- Wetland Coniferous Forest -Tidal
- Wetland Coniferous - Diked
- Upland Shrub-Scrub
- Wetland Shrub-Scrub - Non Tidal
- Wetland Shrub-Scrub - Tidal
- Wetland Shrub-Scrub - Diked
- Upland Herbaceous
- Wetland Herbaceous - Non Tidal
- Wetland Herbaceous - Tidal
- Wetland Herbaceous - Diked
- Aquatic Beds
- Agriculture
- Tree Farms
- Bare
- Mud
- Sand
- Rock
- Urban
- Water
- Open Spaced - Developed

N

0   2.5   5   10 Kilometers

Columbia River Estuary Ecosystem Classification
Level 6 Primary Cover Class

Map created by K. Marcoe, Lower Columbia River Estuary Partnership;
D.W. Heatwole and C.A. Simenstad, University of Washington,
School of Aquatic & Fishery Sciences

Figure 7. Classification Level 6-Primary Cover Class illustrated for Hydrogeomorphic Reach F (see fig. 4) based on 2010 LCRE Land Cover Classification. The classification encompassed the slightly larger area of the earlier tentative Hydrogeomorphic Reach boundary as shown in figure 4.

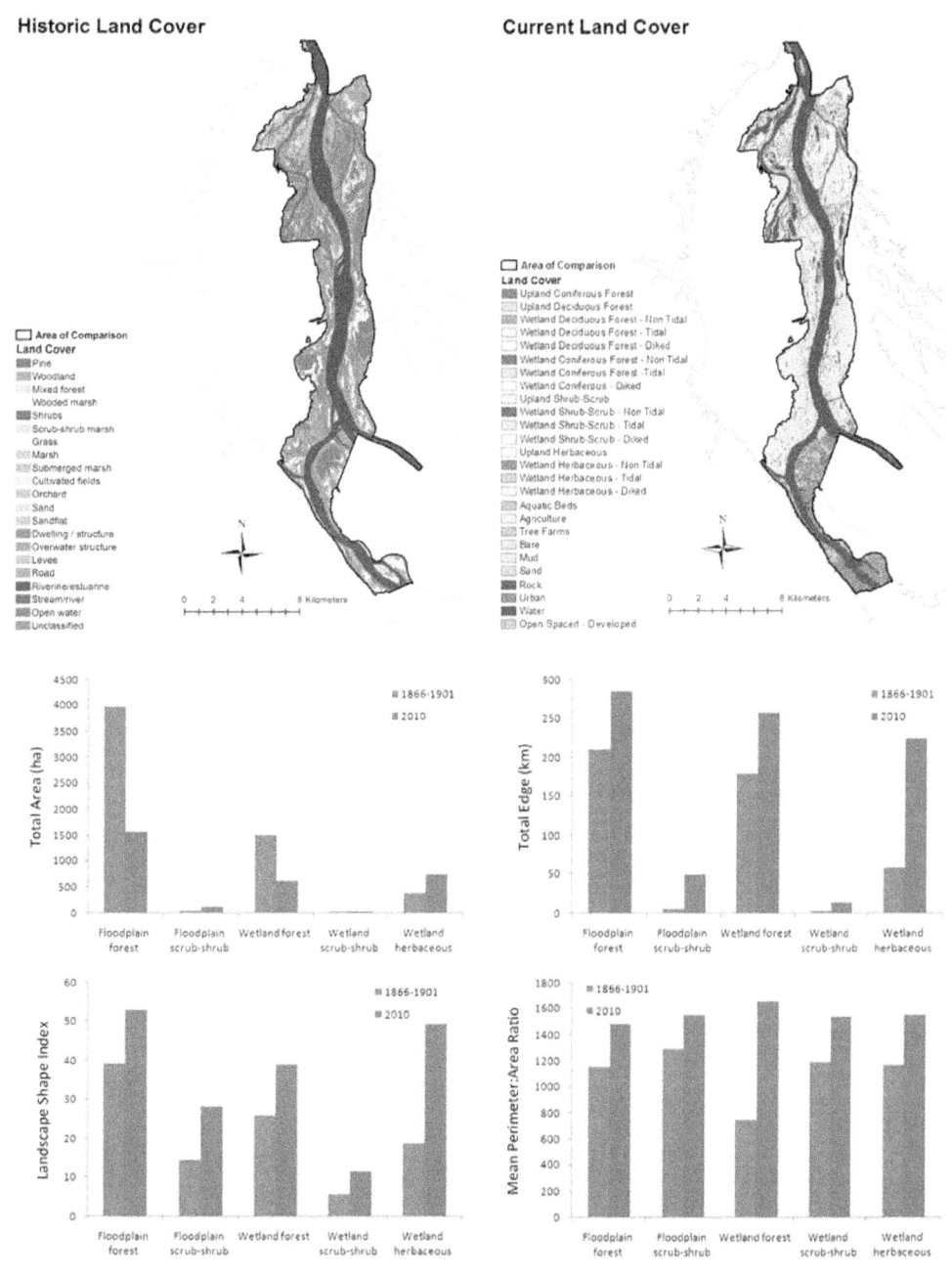

Figure 8. Comparison of Primary Cover Class in Hydrogeomorphic Reach F of Columbia River estuary between 1866 and 1901 (top left; based on analysis of USCGS 't-sheet' survey data; table 1) and 2010 (top right; see Ecosystem Complex under Results, above). FRAGSTATS (McGarigal and Marks, 1995) metrics are generated for land cover vegetation classes as landscape patches illustrate in the lower panels (a, middle left) total area, (b, middle right) total edge, (c, lower left) shape index, and (d, lower right) perimeter:area ratio.

Table 1. Sources and attributes of spatial data used to develop draft Columbia River Estuary Ecosystem Classification.

[rkm 75 = rm 46, rkKm 214 = rm 133, rkm 230 = rm 145]

Data type	Year	Spatial extent	Resolution	Data sources	Online availabil ty
				Land cover	
Land cover	2000	rkm 0– 230	30-m	Landsat 7 Themat c Mapper imagery	http://edcsns17.cr.usgs.gov/NewEarthExplorer/
Wetlands	1974	rkm 0230	1:24,000	U.S. Fish and Wildlife Service National Wetland _nventory	http://www fws.gov/wetlands/Data/
Aerial imagery	2009	rkm 0–230	1-m	U.S. Department of Agriculture digital orthophotographs	http://datagateway nrcs.usda.gov/
Ecoregions	1984–2007	RKm 0 to 230	varies	U.S. Environmental Protection Agency ecoregion classification	http://www.epa.gov/wed/pages/ecoregions htm
				Bathymetry	
Bathymetry	varies	RKm 0 to 230	varies	Lower Columbia River Estuary Partnership bathymetry compilation	http://lcrep.org/
Historical Bathymetry	1866 to 1901	RKm 0 to 214	1:10,000 to 1:20,000	U.S. Coast and Geodetic Survey hydrographic maps, provided by National Oceanographic and Atmospheric Administration Coastal Services Center	https://catalyst.uw.edu/workspace/wet/14965/82924

48

Table 1. Sources and attributes of spatial data used to develop draft Columbia River Estuary Ecosystem Classification.—Continued

				Topography	
Topography and cultural features	varies	RKm 0 to 230	1:24,000	U.S. Geological Survey topographic maps	http://edcsns17.cr.usgs.gov/NewEarthExplorer/
Historical Topography and Land Cover	1866 to 1901	RKm 0 to 214	1:10,000	U.S. Coast and Geodetic Survey topographic maps, provided by National Oceanographic and Atmospheric Administration Coastal Services Center	https://catalyst.uw.edu/workspace/wet/14965/82924
Elevation	varies	RKm 0 to 230	10-m	U.S. Geological Survey National Elevation Dataset	http://ned.usgs.gov/
Elevation	2010	RKm 0 to 230	1-m	U.S. Army Corps of Engineers LiDAR survey	https://www.nwp.usace.army.mil/services/home.asp
Hydrology	varies	RKm 0 to 230	30-m	Earth Design Consultants, Inc. flood-plain extent	
				Geology and soils	
Soils	varies	RKm 0 to 230	varies	Natural Resources Conservation Service (NRCS)	http://datagateway.nrcs.usda.gov
Geology	varies	RKm 0 to 230, Oregon only	varies	Oregon Department of Geology and Mineral Industries statewide geologic map	http://spatialdata.oregonexplorer.info
Geology	varies	RKm 0 to 230, Washington only	1:100,000	Washington State Department of Natural Resources Division of Geology and Earth Resources statewide geologic map	http://www.dnr.wa.gov/ResearchScience/Topics/GeosciencesData/Pages/gis_data.aspx
Geology	varies	RKm 122 to 150, 185 to 206	1:24,000	U.S. Geological Survey geologic maps	http://ngmdb.usgs.gov/

Table 2. Preliminary list of ecosystem complexes mapped under Level 4 of the Columbia River Estuary Ecosystem Classification.

Complex	Brief description
Aquatic complexes	
backwater embayment	large indentations of the shoreline, connected by a smaller opening or slough
embayment	large, open indentations of the shoreline
primary channel	primary channel of river
tributary channel	larger river tributaries
tributary secondary channel	channel beginning in a tributary and connected to a larger channel at both ends at least seasonally
Flood-plain complexes	
bedrock	bedrock above surface of flood plain
developed	areas where flood plain is completely obscured by development
dune deposit	accumulation of wind-blown sediment
flood plain	undifferentiated Holocene flood plain
flood plain backswamp	low areas away from primary channel, generally with many wetlands and lakes
flood plain bar and scroll	bar and swale topography
landslide	deposits and associated topography resulting from mass movements
secondary channel	channel that is connected to primary channel at both ends at least seasonally
terrace	pre-Holocene alluvial deposit surrounded by Holocene flood plain or elevated Holocene flood plain surfaces above historically active flood plain
tributary fan	alluvial fans at mouths of tributaries
tributary flood plain	flood plains of tributaries

Table 3. Preliminary list of geomorphic catenae mapped under Level 5 of the Columbia River Estuary Ecosystem Classification.

Catena	Brief description
Aquatic catenae	
deep channel	deepest part of channel
intermittently exposed	sparsely vegetated beaches and shallow water areas within channels
permanently flooded	permanently flooded part of channel, excluding the deepest part
side channel	secondary or distributary channels on major tributaries, for which there is no bathymetric data
unknown depth	channel areas lacking bathymetric data
Flood-plain catenae	
artificial beach/bar	beach resulting from anthropogenic activity
artificial water body	undifferentiated artificial water body
bedrock	bedrock above surface of flood plain
crevasse splay	lacustrine delta deposit that is not from a channel originating outside the flood plain
developed flood plain	areas where flood plain is completely obscured by development
dune deposit	accumulation of wind-blown sediment
filled areas	filled in areas; generally are shallow water or islands on historic maps, includes dredge spoils.
flood plain	undifferentiated flood plain
flood-plain channel island	islands in flood-plain channels
flood-plain channel	channels that do not originate outside the flood plain and are not connected to a primary channel at both ends
lake or wetland	low areas that cannot be resolved as wetland or lake/pond, generally are drained lakes.
lake/pond	bodies of water, generally not channelized, includes cut off channels and seasonally inundated areas.
lake/pond island	island in a non-channelized water body
landslide deposit	mass-wasting deposit on flood plain
natural levee	ridges from lateral migration of channels, may include shallow swales where ridges coalesce and ridge/swale distinction is ambiguous; often are sub-parallel to a present or former channel.

Table 3. Preliminary list of geomorphic catenae mapped under Level 5 of the Columbia River Estuary Ecosystem Classification.—Continued

Catena	Brief description
Flood-plain catenae—Continued	
terrace	pre-Holocene alluvial deposit surrounded by Holocene flood plain or elevated Holocene flood plain surfaces above historically active flood plain
tributary (minor)	tributary channels of smaller streams
tributary fan	alluvial fans at mouths of tributaries
tributary valley (outside flood plain)	low parts of tributary valleys that extend outside the Holocene flood plain
unknown	insufficient information to permit classification
wetland	low relatively flat areas in flood plain that are or historically were seasonally inundated
Flood-plain modifier	
Artificial	completely artificial feature
Altered	feature whose geometry has changed because of anthropogenic activity
Altered hydrology	feature whose hydrology has changed because of anthropogenic activity
Diked	area not hydrologically connected with primary channel because of dike
Partially diked	area of limited hydrologic connection with primary channel because of dike

Table 4. Classification hierarchy in relation to geology, time and human disturbances.

Classification level	Main geologic controls and major (including anthropogenic) events	Temporal scales	Potential application to management and restoration
Ecosystem Province	Plate tectonics, global continental position, and topography	50-250 Ma	Flow and sediment transport, alteration by basin-wide flow regulation, land-use practices, and sensitivity to global climate change vary by province.
Ecoregion	Formation and uplift of Cascade and Coast Ranges, subsidence of Portland Basin	1-50 Ma	Flow and sediment transport, alteration by basin-wide flow regulation, land-use practices, and sensitivity to global climate change vary by ecoregion.
Hydrogeomorphic Reach	Establishment of Columbia River drainage, Columbia River Basalt flows, Columbia River aggradation since last glacial maximum	0.01-20 Ma	Flow and sediment transport, alteration by basin-wide flow regulation, land-use practices, sensitivity to global climate change vary by hydrogeomorphic reach.
Ecosystem Complex	Holocene aggradation and Columbia River sediment transport since last glacial maximum sea-level low, episodic volcanogenic sediment inputs, landslides, land-use changes, engineering effects including dam construction, bank stabilization, levee construction, channel dredging.	20-10,000 yrs	Information to guide management and restoration actions including siting of conservation easements/purchases, levee setbacks, altered dredging strategies, and flow-regime restoration.
Geomorphic Catena	Columbia River floods, sediment transport processes, episodic subsidence and tectonic warping associated with Cascadia earthquake cycle since sea- level stabilization, land-use changes, engineering effects including dam construction, bank stabilization, levee construction, channel dredging.	1-2,000 yrs	Information to guide management and restoration actions including siting of conservation easements/purchases, levee setbacks, altered dredging strategies, and flow-regime restoration.
Primary Land Cover	Columbia River flow, sediment transport and tidal processes, land-use changes, engineering effects including dam construction, bank stabilization, levee construction, channel dredging.	hours to 100 yrs	Information to guide management and restoration actions including siting of conservation easements/purchases, levee setbacks, altered dredging strategies, restoration of native species, control of invasive species, and flow-regime restoration.

53